SCOTT FORESMAN
Reading Street
COMMON CORE

Reading Street Common Core
Writing to Sources

Glenview, Illinois

Boston, Massachusetts

Chandler, Arizona

Upper Saddle River, New Jersey

D1313641

PEARSON

ISBN-13: 978-0-328-76857-8
ISBN-10:   0-328-76857-X

1 2 3 4 5 6 7 8 9 10 VON4 16 15 14 13 12

Reading Street Common Core Writing to Sources makes fact-finding fun! Students substantiate their claims and communicate in writing what they have learned from one text and then from other related texts.

Reading Street Common Core Writing to Sources encourages students to collaborate and share their growing knowledge with peers, adding quality experiences in the art of using text-based evidence.

Reading Street Common Core Writing to Sources provides more practice with all modes of writing—argument, informative/explanatory, and narrative—and connects to the Common Core State Standards.

Reading Street Common Core Writing to Sources gives students opportunities to complete Performance Tasks by writing in response to what they read and collaborating with others.

Reading Street Common Core Writing to Sources offers you an alternative approach to writing tasks on Reading Street!

1 Write Like a Reporter
Write to one source.
Students respond to the main selection by citing evidence from the text.

2 Connect the Texts
Write to two sources.
Students respond to the main and paired selections by citing evidence from the texts.

3 Prove It! Unit Writing Task
Write to multiple sources.
Students analyze multiple sources within a unit and cite evidence from the texts.

4 More Connect the Texts
Additional lessons specific to writing forms within all modes of writing—argument, informative/explanatory, and narrative—are included.

"Write Like a Reporter!"

Table of Contents

Get Ready for Performance Tasks

More Connect the Texts 197

Unit 1 Living and Learning

Writing Focus: Narrative

Write Like a Reporter
Narrative Paragraph

Student Prompt Reread pp. 41–43 of *When Charlie McButton Lost Power.* Make inferences about the characters Charlie and Isabel Jane based on evidence in the text. Use these inferences as you write a story about Charlie and Isabel Jane and what they do together the next day. Make sure the events in your story follow logically from the events in the poem.

_____

_____

_____

_____

_____

_____

_____

_____

_____

_____

_____

_____

_____

_____

_____

_____

_____

Write Like a Reporter
Narrative Paragraph

> **Student Prompt, p. 6** Reread pp. 41–43 of *When Charlie McButton Lost Power.* Make inferences about the characters Charlie and Isabel Jane based on evidence in the text. Use these inferences as you write a story about Charlie and Isabel Jane and what they do together the next day. Make sure the events in your story follow logically from the events in the poem.

Writing to Sources Explain to students that an inference is a conclusion we draw based on information we find in a text. Point out that to make and support valid inferences about the characters in *When Charlie McButton Lost Power,* students will need to reread the text, looking closely at what the author has the characters say and do. Tell students they should use their inferences to support their characterizations as they write a new narrative that extends the storyline.

Students' stories should:

- show knowledge of the poem's characters, setting, and plot
- develop imagined experiences in a clear event sequence
- use dialogue and descriptions to show responses of characters to a new situation
- demonstrate strong command of the conventions of standard written English

ⓒ Common Core State Standards

Writing 3. Write narratives to develop real or imagined experiences or events using effective technique, descriptive details, and clear event sequences.

Connect the Texts
Narrative Conversation

Student Prompt Look back at *When Charlie McButton Lost Power* and "How a Kite Changed the World." Imagine that Charlie McButton meets Benjamin Franklin. What do you think Charlie would say to Franklin? Use evidence from both texts, as well as inferences you have made about both characters, to write a story about their meeting. Include a conversation in which Charlie tells why electricity is important to him and Franklin responds.

_____

_____

_____

_____

_____

_____

_____

_____

_____

_____

_____

_____

_____

_____

Connect the Texts
Narrative Conversation

Student Prompt, p. 8 Look back at *When Charlie McButton Lost Power* and "How a Kite Changed the World." Imagine that Charlie McButton meets Benjamin Franklin. What do you think Charlie would say to Franklin? Use evidence from both texts, as well as inferences you have made about both characters, to write a story about their meeting. Include a conversation in which Charlie tells why electricity is important to him and Franklin responds.

Writing to Sources Discuss students' inferences about Charlie McButton and Benjamin Franklin. Ask students to cite evidence from the texts that supports their inferences and proves they are valid. Suggest that students listen to real conversations to use as models for the imagined conversation they write in their narrative.

		4-point Narrative Writing Rubric			
Score	**Narrative Focus**	**Organization**	**Development of Narrative**	**Language and Vocabulary**	**Conventions**
4	Narrative is clearly focused and developed throughout.	Narrative has a well-developed, logical, easy-to-follow plot.	Narrative includes thorough and effective use of details, dialogue, and description.	Narrative uses precise, concrete sensory language as well as figurative language and/or domain-specific vocabulary.	Narrative has correct grammar, usage, spelling, capitalization, and punctuation.
3	Narrative is mostly focused and developed throughout.	Narrative has a plot, but there may be some lack of clarity and/or unrelated events.	Narrative includes adequate use of details, dialogue and description.	Narrative uses adequate sensory and figurative language and/or domain-specific vocabulary.	Narrative has a few errors but is completely understandable.
2	Narrative is somewhat developed but may occasionally lose focus.	Narrative's plot is difficult to follow, and ideas are not connected well.	Narrative includes only a few details, dialogues, and descriptions.	Language in narrative is not precise or sensory; lacks domain-specific vocabulary.	Narrative has some errors in usage, grammar, spelling and/or punctuation.
1	Narrative may be confusing, unfocused, or too short.	Narrative has little or no apparent plot.	Narrative includes few or no details, dialogue or description.	Language in narrative is vague, unclear, or confusing.	Narrative is hard to follow because of frequent errors.
0	Narrative gets no credit if it does not demonstrate adequate command of narrative writing traits.				

Ⓒ Common Core State Standards

Writing 3. Write narratives to develop real or imagined experiences or events using effective technique, descriptive details, and clear event sequences.

Write Like a Reporter
Narrative Paragraph

Student Prompt Reread pp. 73–75 of *What About Me?* Use what you read and inferred from the text about these characters and events to write a story in which the merchant's daughter is the main character. Tell about what she is doing before the young man comes to her village and what happens after she goes with him to the other village.

_____

_____

_____

_____

_____

_____

_____

_____

_____

_____

_____

_____

_____

_____

_____

_____

_____

Write Like a Reporter
Narrative Paragraph

> **Student Prompt, p. 10** Reread pp. 73–75 of *What About Me?* Use what you read and inferred from the text about these characters and events to write a story in which the merchant's daughter is the main character. Tell about what she is doing before the young man comes to her village and what happens after she goes with him to the other village.

Writing to Sources Remind students that they will need to look closely at the words and the phrases the author uses in order to make inferences about the characters' personalities and feelings. Students can use these inferences to ensure that the characters act and talk in their story as they did in the fable. Discuss with students the events from the fable that will occur in the middle part of their story.

Students' stories should:

- show knowledge of the fable's characters and plot
- combine events from the fable with imagined events in a new event sequence
- use dialogue and descriptions to develop new events in the plot
- demonstrate strong command of the conventions of standard written English

---

© Common Core State Standards

Writing 3. Write narratives to develop real or imagined experiences or events using effective technique, descriptive details, and clear event sequences.

Connect the Texts
Narrative Fantasy

Student Prompt Look back at *What About Me?* and "How the Desert Tortoise Got Its Shell." How do the young man and Desert Tortoise use cooperation to get what they want? Write a fantasy in which the young man and Desert Tortoise work together to achieve a goal. Use evidence from both texts, as well as your inferences about both characters, as you write your fantasy.

_____

_____

_____

_____

_____

_____

_____

_____

_____

_____

_____

_____

_____

_____

_____

_____

_____

Connect the Texts
Narrative Fantasy

Student Prompt, p. 12 Look back at *What About Me?* and "How the Desert Tortoise Got Its Shell." How do the young man and Desert Tortoise use cooperation to get what they want? Write a fantasy in which the young man and Desert Tortoise work together to achieve a goal. Use evidence from both texts, as well as your inferences about both characters, as you write your fantasy.

Writing to Sources Discuss details in both texts and inferences students made about the two characters. Have students cite evidence from the texts that supports their inferences. Ask them how they can use the details and inferences when planning their fantasy. If necessary, brainstorm possible events for the new story about the young man and Desert Tortoise and list the events on the board.

	4-point Narrative Writing Rubric				
Score	**Narrative Focus**	**Organization**	**Development of Narrative**	**Language and Vocabulary**	**Conventions**
4	Narrative is clearly focused and developed throughout.	Narrative has a well-developed, logical, easy-to-follow plot.	Narrative includes thorough and effective use of details, dialogue, and description.	Narrative uses precise, concrete sensory language as well as figurative language and/or domain-specific vocabulary.	Narrative has correct grammar, usage, spelling, capitalization, and punctuation.
3	Narrative is mostly focused and developed throughout.	Narrative has a plot, but there may be some lack of clarity and/or unrelated events.	Narrative includes adequate use of details, dialogue and description.	Narrative uses adequate sensory and figurative language and/or domain-specific vocabulary.	Narrative has a few errors but is completely understandable.
2	Narrative is somewhat developed but may occasionally lose focus.	Narrative's plot is difficult to follow, and ideas are not connected well.	Narrative includes only a few details, dialogues, and descriptions.	Language in narrative is not precise or sensory; lacks domain-specific vocabulary.	Narrative has some errors in usage, grammar, spelling and/or punctuation.
1	Narrative may be confusing, unfocused, or too short.	Narrative has little or no apparent plot.	Narrative includes few or no details, dialogue or description.	Language in narrative is vague, unclear, or confusing.	Narrative is hard to follow because of frequent errors.
0	Narrative gets no credit if it does not demonstrate adequate command of narrative writing traits.				

Ⓒ **Common Core State Standards**

Writing 3. Write narratives to develop real or imagined experiences or events using effective technique, descriptive details, and clear event sequences.

Write Like a Reporter
Narrative Paragraph

Student Prompt Reread pp. 108–113 of *Kumak's Fish*. How do you know that this story is a tall tale? Look for evidence in this part of the text. Then rewrite this part so that the story is realistic fiction and not a tall tale.

_____

_____

_____

_____

_____

_____

_____

_____

_____

_____

_____

_____

_____

_____

_____

_____

_____

_____

Write Like a Reporter
Narrative Paragraph

> **Student Prompt, p. 14** Reread pp. 108–113 of *Kumak's Fish*. How do you
> know that this story is a tall tale? Look for evidence in this part of the text. Then
> rewrite this part so that the story is realistic fiction and not a tall tale.

Writing to Sources Review the similarities and differences between tall tales and
realistic fiction with students. Suggest that when they look for words and events that
identify the text as a tall tale, they list what they find. This will help them recognize
what they need to change as they rewrite the last six pages to make the tall tale into
realistic fiction.

Students' revised story parts should:

- reveal their understanding of the differences between tall tales and realistic
  fiction
- use details, dialogue, and descriptions to develop the story events
- provide a sense of closure
- demonstrate strong command of the conventions of standard written English

---

© Common Core State Standards

Writing 3. Write narratives to develop real or imagined experiences or events using effective technique, descriptive details, and clear event
sequences.

Connect the Texts
Narrative Story

> **Student Prompt** Look back at *Kumak's Fish* and "How to Catch a Fish."
> Imagine Kumak and Vicki Edwards go fishing together. Use evidence from
> both texts, as well as inferences you made about both characters, to write a
> story about what happens. Include a conversation in which they talk about
> their favorite fishing methods.

_____

_____

_____

_____

_____

_____

_____

_____

_____

_____

_____

_____

_____

_____

Connect the Texts
Narrative Story

Student Prompt, p. 16 Look back at *Kumak's Fish* and "How to Catch a Fish." Imagine Kumak and Vicki Edwards go fishing together. Use evidence from both texts, as well as inferences you made about both characters, to write a story about what happens. Include a conversation in which they talk about their favorite fishing methods.

Writing to Sources Point out that to make and support valid inferences about the characters in the two selections, students will need to reread the texts, looking closely at what the authors have the characters say and do. Tell students they should use their inferences to support their characterizations. Remind them to look for details about fishing methods to use in their stories.

	4-point Narrative Writing Rubric				
Score	**Narrative Focus**	**Organization**	**Development of Narrative**	**Language and Vocabulary**	**Conventions**
4	Narrative is clearly focused and developed throughout.	Narrative has a well-developed, logical, easy-to-follow plot.	Narrative includes thorough and effective use of details, dialogue, and description.	Narrative uses precise, concrete sensory language as well as figurative language and/or domain-specific vocabulary.	Narrative has correct grammar, usage, spelling, capitalization, and punctuation.
3	Narrative is mostly focused and developed throughout.	Narrative has a plot, but there may be some lack of clarity and/or unrelated events.	Narrative includes adequate use of details, dialogue and description.	Narrative uses adequate sensory and figurative language and/or domain-specific vocabulary.	Narrative has a few errors but is completely understandable.
2	Narrative is somewhat developed but may occasionally lose focus.	Narrative's plot is difficult to follow, and ideas are not connected well.	Narrative includes only a few details, dialogues, and descriptions.	Language in narrative is not precise or sensory; lacks domain-specific vocabulary.	Narrative has some errors in usage, grammar, spelling and/or punctuation.
1	Narrative may be confusing, unfocused, or too short.	Narrative has little or no apparent plot.	Narrative includes few or no details, dialogue or description.	Language in narrative is vague, unclear, or confusing.	Narrative is hard to follow because of frequent errors.
0	Narrative gets no credit if it does not demonstrate adequate command of narrative writing traits.				

© **Common Core State Standards**

Writing 3. Write narratives to develop real or imagined experiences or events using effective technique, descriptive details, and clear event sequences.

Write Like a Reporter
Narrative Paragraph

Student Prompt Reread pp. 141–145 of *Supermarket*. Write a realistic story in which you shop at this supermarket. Tell what you buy in each section of the supermarket featured on these pages. Use details from the text and illustrations in your story. Include sensory details to help readers better visualize the experience.

_____

_____

_____

_____

_____

_____

_____

_____

_____

_____

_____

_____

_____

_____

_____

_____

_____

Write Like a Reporter
Narrative Paragraph

> **Student Prompt, p. 18** Reread pages 141–145 of *Supermarket.* Write a realistic story in which you shop at this supermarket. Tell what you buy in each section of the supermarket featured on these pages. Use details from the text and illustrations in your story. Include sensory details to help readers better visualize the experience.

Writing to Sources Remind students that a narrative recounts events in a clear sequence. Point out that they are to use the text organization of the selection to organize the sequence of events in their story. Suggest that they use time-order words to make the sequence clear and selection and sensory details to make the events realistic.

Students' stories should:

- use the setting of the selection as their story setting
- recount events in a clear sequence
- use time-order words and phrases to signal event order and descriptive details to develop experiences and events
- demonstrate strong command of the conventions of standard written English

© Common Core State Standards

Writing 3. Write narratives to develop real or imagined experiences or events using effective technique, descriptive details, and clear event sequences.

Connect the Texts
Narrative Fantasy

Student Prompt Review "Money from Long Ago" and the items that were once used as money. Write a fantasy about a supermarket that accepts those items as money instead of bills and coins. Use details from *Supermarket* to describe the setting. Tell what happens when people try to buy things at this store.

_____

_____

_____

_____

_____

_____

_____

_____

_____

_____

_____

_____

_____

_____

_____

_____

_____

Connect the Texts
Narrative Fantasy

Student Prompt, p. 20 Review "Money from Long Ago" and the items that were once used as money. Write a fantasy about a supermarket that accepts those items as money instead of bills and coins. Use details from *Supermarket* to describe the setting. Tell what happens when people try to buy things at this store.

Writing to Sources Suggest that as students review the texts, they take notes about the supermarket and the items once used as money. They will use these details as they write their fantasy. Remind students that a fantasy has characters, settings, and/or events that do not exist or occur in real life.

		4-point Narrative Writing Rubric			
Score	**Narrative Focus**	**Organization**	**Development of Narrative**	**Language and Vocabulary**	**Conventions**
4	Narrative is clearly focused and developed throughout.	Narrative has a well-developed, logical, easy-to-follow plot.	Narrative includes thorough and effective use of details, dialogue, and description.	Narrative uses precise, concrete sensory language as well as figurative language and/or domain-specific vocabulary.	Narrative has correct grammar, usage, spelling, capitalization, and punctuation.
3	Narrative is mostly focused and developed throughout.	Narrative has a plot, but there may be some lack of clarity and/or unrelated events.	Narrative includes adequate use of details, dialogue and description.	Narrative uses adequate sensory and figurative language and/or domain-specific vocabulary.	Narrative has a few errors but is completely understandable.
2	Narrative is somewhat developed but may occasionally lose focus.	Narrative's plot is difficult to follow, and ideas are not connected well.	Narrative includes only a few details, dialogues, and descriptions.	Language in narrative is not precise or sensory; lacks domain-specific vocabulary.	Narrative has some errors in usage, grammar, spelling and/or punctuation.
1	Narrative may be confusing, unfocused, or too short.	Narrative has little or no apparent plot.	Narrative includes few or no details, dialogue or description.	Language in narrative is vague, unclear, or confusing.	Narrative is hard to follow because of frequent errors.
0	Narrative gets no credit if it does not demonstrate adequate command of narrative writing traits.				

© Common Core State Standards

Writing 3. Write narratives to develop real or imagined experiences or events using effective technique, descriptive details, and clear event sequences.

Write Like a Reporter
Narrative Paragraph

Student Prompt Reread pp. 180–181 of *My Rows and Piles of Coins*.
Imagine a scene in which Yeyo and Murete plan the surprise for Saruni.
Use text details and your inferences about these characters as you write the
dialogue and narration for the scene.

_____

_____

_____

_____

_____

_____

_____

_____

_____

_____

_____

_____

_____

_____

_____

Narrative Paragraph

> **Student Prompt, p. 22** Reread pp. 180–181 of *My Rows and Piles of Coins.*
> Imagine a scene in which Yeyo and Murete plan the surprise for Saruni. Use text
> details and your inferences about these characters as you write the dialogue
> and narration for the scene.

Writing to Sources Remind students that dialogue reveals details about characters
and plot through conversation, and narration gives details that cannot be given in
dialogue. Have students review the text, looking for details about the two characters
that will help them write their story scene.

Students' scenes should:

- show knowledge of the story's characters and plot
- fit logically into the established plot
- use dialogue and narration to reveal characters' thoughts and feelings and
  advance the plot
- demonstrate strong command of the conventions of standard written English

---

© Common Core State Standards

Writing 3. Write narratives to develop real or imagined experiences or events using effective technique, descriptive details, and clear event
sequences.

Connect the Texts
Narrative Dialogue

Student Prompt Imagine that you and Saruni from *My Rows and Piles of Coins* are friends. Write a story in which Saruni asks you how he can save money to buy a cart. What advice would you give him? Use information from the Web site in "Learning About Money."

_____

_____

_____

_____

_____

_____

_____

_____

_____

_____

_____

_____

_____

_____

_____

Connect the Texts
Narrative Dialogue

Student Prompt, p. 24 Imagine that you and Saruni from *My Rows and Piles of Coins* are friends. Write a story in which Saruni asks you how he can save money to buy a cart. What advice would you give him? Use information from the Web site in "Learning About Money."

Writing to Sources Have students return to the texts, looking for details about the character and events in the story and for information about saving on the Web site. Point out that students will use the details and information in their story. Suggest that they use dialogue they see in the story as a model for any dialogue they decide to write.

			4-point Narrative Writing Rubric		
Score	**Narrative Focus**	**Organization**	**Development of Narrative**	**Language and Vocabulary**	**Conventions**
4	Narrative is clearly focused and developed throughout.	Narrative has a well-developed, logical, easy-to-follow plot.	Narrative includes thorough and effective use of details, dialogue, and description.	Narrative uses precise, concrete sensory language as well as figurative language and/or domain-specific vocabulary.	Narrative has correct grammar, usage, spelling, capitalization, and punctuation.
3	Narrative is mostly focused and developed throughout.	Narrative has a plot, but there may be some lack of clarity and/or unrelated events.	Narrative includes adequate use of details, dialogue and description.	Narrative uses adequate sensory and figurative language and/or domain-specific vocabulary.	Narrative has a few errors but is completely understandable.
2	Narrative is somewhat developed but may occasionally lose focus.	Narrative's plot is difficult to follow, and ideas are not connected well.	Narrative includes only a few details, dialogues, and descriptions.	Language in narrative is not precise or sensory; lacks domain-specific vocabulary.	Narrative has some errors in usage, grammar, spelling and/or punctuation.
1	Narrative may be confusing, unfocused, or too short.	Narrative has little or no apparent plot.	Narrative includes few or no details, dialogue or description.	Language in narrative is vague, unclear, or confusing.	Narrative is hard to follow because of frequent errors.
0	Narrative gets no credit if it does not demonstrate adequate command of narrative writing traits.				

© Common Core State Standards

Writing 3. Write narratives to develop real or imagined experiences or events using effective technique, descriptive details, and clear event sequences.

Prove It!
Personal Narrative

Academic Vocabulary

A **personal narrative** is a first-person account in which the writer tells about an event, incident, or experience in his or her own life.

ELL

Introduce Genre Write *personal* on the board and explain that this word describes anything relating to an individual or a person. Write *narrative* and explain this is another word for *story.* Help students understand that a personal narrative is simply a story about the writer. Discuss with students the key features of a personal narrative that appear on this page.

Achieving a Goal

Personal Narrative

In this unit, students have read examples of narrative writing, including a poem, a fable, a thank-you note, a description, and realistic fiction, and have had the opportunity to write in this mode. Remind students of texts and writing tasks (such as Write Like a Reporter and Connect the Texts) in which they have encountered and practiced narrative writing.

Key Features of a Personal Narrative

- tells about an experience
- organizes events in a sequence that unfolds naturally
- includes the writer's actions, thoughts, feelings, and opinions about the experience
- uses time-order words and phrases to signal event order
- provides descriptive details that make the experience vivid for readers
- uses the first-person pronouns *I, me,* and *my* or *we, us,* and *our*
- provides a sense of closure

Writing Task Overview

Each unit writing task provides students with an opportunity to write to sources. To successfully complete the task, students must analyze, synthesize, and evaluate multiple complex texts and create their own written response.

Achieving a Goal

Part 1: Students will read and take notes on the selected sources. They will then respond to several questions about these sources and discuss their written responses with partners or in small groups.

Part 2: Students will work individually to plan, write, and revise their own personal narrative.

Scorable Products: evidence-based short responses, personal narrative

Achieving a Goal: Writing Task – Short Response

Teacher Directions:

1. Introduce the Sources Refer students to the following texts in the Student Edition:

1. *What About Me?*, pp. 64–77

2. *Kumak's Fish*, pp. 98–113

3. *My Rows and Piles of Coins*, pp. 168–183

Explain to students that they will need to draw evidence and support from the texts above in order to answer evidence-based short response questions and to write a personal narrative. Students should take notes and categorize information as they closely reread the texts. Students should be given paper or a relevant graphic organizer from the TR DVD for note-taking.

2. Provide Student Directions and Scoring Information (p. 30) Answer any task-related questions students may have. If necessary, provide additional paper for students to write their responses.

3. Initiate the Writing Task If you are timing this part of the task, you may wish to alert students when half the allotted time has elapsed and again when 5 minutes remain.

4. Facilitate Collaboration After students have completed their written responses to the evidence-based short response questions, assign partners or small groups and have them discuss their responses. If students struggle to work together productively, provide them with tips and strategies for expressing their ideas and building on others'.

© **Common Core State Standards**

Writing 3. Write narratives to develop real or imagined experiences or events using effective technique, descriptive details, and clear event sequences. **Writing 8.** Recall information from experiences or gather information from print and digital sources; take brief notes on sources and sort evidence into provided categories. **Speaking/Listening 1.** Engage effectively in a range of collaborative discussions (one-on-one, in groups, and teacher-led) with diverse partners on grade 3 topics and texts, building on others' ideas and expressing their own clearly. **(Also Writing 3.a., Writing 3.b., Writing 3.c., Writing 3.d.)**

Scoring Information

Use the following 2-point scoring rubrics to evaluate students' answers to the evidence-based short response questions.

1. Compare characters' goals and ways they achieve those goals. How are the goals and the ways the characters achieve them similar and different?

	Analysis Rubric
2	The response: • demonstrates the ability to analyze similarities and differences among the texts • includes specific details that make reference to the texts
1	The response: • demonstrates a limited ability to analyze similarities and differences among the texts • includes some details that make reference to the texts
0	A response receives no credit if it demonstrates no ability to analyze similarities and differences among the texts or includes no relevant details from the texts.

2. If you were telling about what is involved in achieving a goal, what would you say? Cite examples from the texts of what the characters do.

	Synthesis Rubric
2	The response: • demonstrates the ability to synthesize information from the sources in order to describe how to achieve a goal • includes specific details that make reference to the texts
1	The response: • demonstrates a limited ability to synthesize information from the sources in order to describe how to achieve a goal • includes some details that make reference to the texts
0	A response receives no credit if it demonstrates no ability to synthesize information from the sources or includes no relevant details from the texts.

3. Prepare questions that could be used to evaluate whether a goal has been successfully achieved. Use the questions to rate the efforts of each of the main characters in the three texts. Cite examples from the texts.

Evaluation Rubric	
2	The response: • demonstrates the ability to evaluate texts in order to create questions and rate characters' efforts • includes specific details that make reference to the texts
1	The response: • demonstrates a limited ability to evaluate texts in order to create questions and rate characters' efforts • includes some details that make reference to the texts
0	A response receives no credit if it demonstrates no ability to evaluate texts or includes no relevant details from the texts.

ⓒ **Common Core State Standards**

Writing 8. Recall information from experiences or gather information from print and digital sources; take brief notes on sources and sort evidence into provided categories.

Achieving a Goal
Writing Task – Short Response

Student Directions:

Your assignment   You will reread several selections from Unit 1 and take notes on these sources. Then you will answer three questions about these materials. You may refer to your notes or to any of the sources as often as you like.

Sources

1. *What About Me?*, pp. 64–77

2. *Kumak's Fish*, pp. 98–113

3. *My Rows and Piles of Coins*, pp. 168–183

Be sure to read closely and take good notes. Your sources and notes will be the basis for writing your own personal narrative in the second part of this writing task.

Evidence-Based Short Response Questions   Answer the short response questions on the lines provided below each question. Your answers to these questions will be scored. Be sure to base your answers on the sources you have just read. Remember that you may refer back to your notes or to any of the sources.

After you have answered the questions, you will discuss your responses with a partner or in a small group. Your teacher will let you know when to begin the discussion part of this task.

Scoring Information   Your responses will be scored based on how you demonstrate your ability to:

- compare and contrast information across texts
- tell how a goal is achieved
- rate the efforts of the characters
- include specific details that clearly reference the sources

Evidence-Based Short Response Questions

1. Compare characters' goals and ways they achieve those goals. How are the goals and the ways the characters achieve them similar and different?

_____

_____

_____

_____

2. If you were telling about what is involved in achieving a goal, what would you say? Cite examples from the texts of what the characters do.

_____

_____

_____

_____

3. Prepare questions that could be used to evaluate whether a goal has been successfully achieved. Use the questions to rate the efforts of each of the main characters in the three texts. Cite examples from the texts.

_____

_____

_____

_____

Collaborative Discussion

After you have written your responses to the questions, discuss your ideas. Your teacher will assign you a partner or a small group and let you know when to begin.

Achieving a Goal: Writing Task – Personal Narrative

Teacher Directions:

1. **Provide Student Directions and Scoring Information (p. 34)** Explain to students that they will now review their notes and sources and plan, draft, and revise their personal narratives. Although they may use their notes and sources, they must work alone. Students will be allowed to look back at the answers they wrote to the short response questions, but they are not allowed to make changes to those answers. Have students read the directions for the personal narrative and answer any task-related questions they may have. Students should be given paper on which to write their personal narratives.

2. **Initiate the Writing Task** If you are timing this part of the task, you may wish to suggest approximate times for students to begin writing and revising. If students wish to continue writing rather than revising, allow them to do so. Alert students when 5 minutes remain.

3. **Scoring Information** Use the scoring rubric on the next page to evaluate students' personal narratives.

4. **Personal Narrative Prompt** Imagine you are one of the characters from *What About Me?, Kumak's Fish,* or *My Rows and Piles of Coins.* Write a personal narrative about another goal you have accomplished. Tell the story of how you achieved this goal. Develop your personal narrative by using what you learned from reading the texts. Be sure to follow the conventions of written English.

4-point Narrative Writing Rubric					
Score	**Narrative Focus**	**Organization**	**Development of Narrative**	**Language and Vocabulary**	**Conventions**
4	Personal narrative is clearly focused and developed throughout.	Personal narrative has a well-developed, logical, easy-to-follow plot.	Personal narrative includes thorough and effective use of details, dialogue, and description.	Personal narrative uses precise, concrete sensory language as well as figurative language and/or domain specific vocabulary.	Personal narrative has correct grammar, usage, spelling, capitalization, and punctuation.
3	Personal narrative is mostly focused and developed throughout.	Personal narrative has a plot, but there may be some lack of clarity and/or unrelated events.	Personal narrative includes adequate use of details, dialogue, and description.	Personal narrative uses adequate sensory and figurative language and/or domain specific vocabulary.	Personal narrative has a few errors but is completely understandable.
2	Personal narrative is somewhat developed but may occasionally lose focus.	Personal narrative's plot is difficult to follow, and ideas are not connected well.	Personal narrative includes only a few details, dialogues, and descriptions.	Language in personal narrative is not precise or sensory; lacks domain specific vocabulary.	Personal narrative has some errors in usage, grammar, spelling, and/or punctuation.
1	Personal narrative may be confusing, unfocused, or too short.	Personal narrative has little or no apparent plot.	Personal narrative includes few or no details, dialogue, and description.	Language in personal narrative is vague, unclear, or confusing.	Personal narrative is hard to follow because of frequent errors.
0	The response shows no evidence of the ability to construct a coherent personal narrative using information from sources.				

Achieving a Goal
Writing Task – Personal Narrative

Student Directions:

Your assignment Now you will review your notes and sources and plan, draft, and revise your personal narrative. While you may use your notes and refer to your sources, you must work on your own. You may also refer to the answers you wrote to earlier questions, but you cannot change those answers.

Personal Narrative Prompt Imagine you are one of the characters from *What About Me?*, *Kumak's Fish*, or *My Rows and Piles of Coins*. Write a personal narrative about another goal you have accomplished. Tell the story of how you achieved this goal. Develop your personal narrative by using what you learned from reading the texts. Be sure to follow the conventions of written English.

Scoring Information Your personal narrative will be assigned a score for

1. **Narrative Focus** – how well you maintain your focus and convey your ideas clearly

2. **Organization** – how well the events flow logically from first to last in a clear event sequence

3. **Development** – how well you develop the real experience or event using descriptive details

4. **Language and Vocabulary** – how well you use time-order words to show sequence

5. **Conventions** – how well you follow the rules of usage, punctuation, capitalization, and spelling

Now begin work on your personal narrative. Try to manage your time carefully so that you can

- plan your personal narrative

- write your personal narrative

- revise and edit for a final draft

Achieving a Goal: Writing Task – Personal Narrative

Teacher Directions:

1. Publish Explain to students that publishing their writing is the last step in the writing process. If time permits, have students review one another's compositions and incorporate any comments their classmates have. Discuss different ways technology can be used to publish writing.

2. Present Students will now have the option to present their personal narratives. Have students read aloud their personal narratives to the class. Use the list below to offer students tips on listening and speaking.

While Listening to a Classmate...

- Listen with care.
- Think of questions to ask.

While Speaking to Classmates...

- Speak at an appropriate pace.
- Speak loudly and clearly.

Things to Do Together...

- Link comments to others' remarks.
- Request more detail or clarification.

Ⓒ **Common Core State Standards**

Writing 6. With guidance and support from adults, use technology to produce and publish writing (using keyboarding skills) as well as to interact and collaborate with others. **Speaking/Listening 4.** Report on a topic or text, tell a story, or recount an experience with appropriate facts and relevant, descriptive details, speaking clearly at an understandable pace.

Unit 2 Smart Solutions

Writing Focus: Argument

Write Like a Reporter
Argumentative Paragraph

Student Prompt Reread the selection *Penguin Chick*. What did you think of this text? Did you like it? Did you dislike it? Write an opinion piece in which you state and defend your opinion of the text. Provide evidence from the text to support your opinion.

_____

_____

_____

_____

_____

_____

_____

_____

_____

_____

_____

_____

_____

_____

_____

_____

Write Like a Reporter
Argumentative Paragraph

Student Prompt, p. 38 Reread the selection *Penguin Chick.* What did you think of this text? Did you like it? Did you dislike it? Write an opinion piece in which you state and defend your opinion of the text. Provide evidence from the text to support your opinion.

Writing to Sources Point out to students that they will need to reread the text carefully, looking for specific words and sentences they can use as evidence to support their opinion. Tell them to first state their opinion clearly and then to provide two or three reasons backed by facts and details and organized to support the purpose of their writing.

Students' paragraphs should:

- state a clear opinion about the topic
- provide reasons to support the opinion
- use evidence from the text to support their reasons
- demonstrate strong command of the conventions of standard written English

© **Common Core State Standards**

Writing 1. Write opinion pieces on topics or texts, supporting a point of view with reasons.

Connect the Texts
Argumentative Opinion Piece

Look back at *Penguin Chick* and "Plants Fitting into Their World." Which do you think have a harder time surviving—the penguin chicks or the plants? Draw a conclusion based on facts in the texts and your inferences from the texts. Write an opinion piece in which you state and defend your conclusion. Provide evidence from both texts to support your opinion.

_____

_____

_____

_____

_____

_____

_____

_____

_____

_____

_____

_____

_____

_____

Connect the Texts
Argumentative Opinion Piece

Student Prompt, p. 40 Look back at *Penguin Chick* and "Plants Fitting into Their World." Which do you think have a harder time surviving—the penguin chicks or the plants? Draw a conclusion based on facts in the texts and your inferences from the texts. Write an opinion piece in which you state and defend your conclusion. Provide evidence from both texts to support your opinion.

Writing to Sources Discuss students' conclusions and why they drew those conclusions. Have them go back into both texts and find specific evidence to support their opinion. Remind students to look closely at the authors' words and phrases and to think about the inferences readers can make from this language.

	4-point Argument Writing Rubric				
Score	Statement of Purpose/Focus	Organization	Development of Evidence	Language and Vocabulary	Conventions
4	Opinion is clearly conveyed and well supported; response is focused.	Organization is clear and effective, creating a sense of cohesion.	Evidence is thorough and persuasive and includes facts and details.	Ideas are clearly and effectively conveyed, using precise language and/or domain-specific vocabulary.	Command of conventions is strongly demonstrated.
3	Opinion is clear, adequately supported; response is generally focused.	Organization is clear, though minor flaws may be present and some ideas may be disconnected.	Evidence is adequate and includes facts and details.	Ideas are adequately conveyed, using both precise and more general language; may include domain-specific vocabulary.	Command of conventions is sufficiently demonstrated.
2	Opinion is somewhat supported; response may lack focus or include unnecessary material.	Organization is inconsistent, and flaws are apparent.	Evidence is uneven or incomplete; insufficient use of facts and details.	Ideas are unevenly conveyed, using overly-simplistic language; lack of domain-specific vocabulary.	Command of conventions is uneven.
1	The response may be confusing, unfocused; opinion not sufficiently supported.	Organization is poor or nonexistent.	Evidence is poor or nonexistent.	Ideas are conveyed in a vague, unclear, or confusing manner.	There is very little command of conventions.
0	The response shows no evidence of the ability to construct a coherent opinion essay using information from sources.				

Ⓒ **Common Core State Standards**

Writing 1. Write opinion pieces on topics or texts, supporting a point of view with reasons.

Write Like a Reporter
Argumentative Paragraph

Student Prompt Reread p. 250 of *I Wanna Iguana*. Alex's mother wonders if Alex is ready to have a pet. What do you think? Write your opinion. Then look through the text for evidence that supports your opinion. Find and write at least three good reasons. Conclude by restating your opinion.

_____

_____

_____

_____

_____

_____

_____

_____

_____

_____

_____

_____

_____

_____

_____

_____

Write Like a Reporter
Argumentative Paragraph

> **Student Prompt, p. 42** Reread p. 250 of *I Wanna Iguana*. Alex's mother wonders if Alex is ready to have a pet. What do you think? Write your opinion. Then look through the text for evidence that supports your opinion. Find and write at least three good reasons. Conclude by restating your opinion.

Writing to Sources Suggest that students begin their opinion pieces by writing their answer to this question: Do you think Alex is ready to have a pet? Then have students look in the text for reasons to support their opinion. If they have difficulty finding evidence in the text, guide them to reread pp. 251–253.

Students' paragraphs should:

- introduce the topic and state their opinion
- use an organizational structure that lists supporting reasons
- provide a concluding statement
- demonstrate strong command of the conventions of standard written English

Writing 1. Write opinion pieces on topics or texts, supporting a point of view with reasons.

Name _____

Connect the Texts
Argumentative Opinion Piece

Student Prompt Look back at the notes in *I Wanna Iguana* and the e-mails in "The Big Soccer Game." Which do you think is the better way to communicate with a family member? How about with friends far away? Why? Write your opinion and use the notes and e-mails in the texts as well as examples from your own experience as evidence to support your opinion.

_____

_____

_____

_____

_____

_____

_____

_____

_____

_____

_____

_____

_____

_____

_____

_____

_____

Connect the Texts
Argumentative Opinion Piece

Student Prompt, p. 44 Look back at the notes in *I Wanna Iguana* and the e-mails in "The Big Soccer Game." Which do you think is the better way to communicate with a family member? How about with friends far away? Why? Write your opinion and use the notes and e-mails in the texts as well as examples from your own experience as evidence to support your opinion.

Writing to Sources Review both selections with students, focusing on the form of communication used in each and the advantages and disadvantages of using that form for specific audiences. Suggest that students list their ideas as a way to help them form their opinion. Then once they have stated their opinion, they can use the lists to choose evidence to support their opinion.

4-point Argument Writing Rubric					
Score	**Statement of Purpose/Focus**	**Organization**	**Development of Evidence**	**Language and Vocabulary**	**Conventions**
4	Opinion is clearly conveyed and well supported; response is focused.	Organization is clear and effective, creating a sense of cohesion.	Evidence is thorough and persuasive, and includes facts and details.	Ideas are clearly and effectively conveyed, using precise language and/or domain-specific vocabulary.	Command of conventions is strongly demonstrated.
3	Opinion is clear, adequately supported; response is generally focused.	Organization is clear, though minor flaws may be present and some ideas may be disconnected.	Evidence is adequate and includes facts and details.	Ideas are adequately conveyed, using both precise and more general language; may include domain-specific vocabulary.	Command of conventions is sufficiently demonstrated.
2	Opinion is somewhat supported; response may lack focus or include unnecessary material.	Organization is inconsistent, and flaws are apparent.	Evidence is uneven or incomplete; insufficient use of facts and details.	Ideas are unevenly conveyed, using overly-simplistic language; lack of domain-specific vocabulary.	Command of conventions is uneven.
1	The response may be confusing, unfocused; opinion not sufficiently supported.	Organization is poor or nonexistent.	Evidence is poor or nonexistent.	Ideas are conveyed in a vague, unclear, or confusing manner.	There is very little command of conventions.
0	The response shows no evidence of the ability to construct a coherent opinion essay using information from sources.				

© **Common Core State Standards**

Writing 1. Write opinion pieces on topics or texts, supporting a point of view with reasons.

Write Like a Reporter
Argumentative Paragraph

Student Prompt Reread pp. 288–289 of *Prudy's Problem and How She Solved It*. What is Prudy's solution to her problem? What do you think would be a better solution? Write your idea. Support it with evidence from the text. Include persuasive words, such as *should, best,* and *important*.

_____

_____

_____

_____

_____

_____

_____

_____

_____

_____

_____

_____

_____

_____

_____

_____

_____

Write Like a Reporter
Argumentative Paragraph

Student Prompt, p. 46 Reread pp. 288–289 of *Prudy's Problem and How She Solved It*. What is Prudy's solution to her problem? What do you think would be a better solution? Write your idea. Support it with evidence from the text. Include persuasive words, such as *should, best,* and *important*.

Writing to Sources Point out to students that when they review the text, they need to evaluate Prudy's solution to her problem and think of a different solution to present. After they explain their idea, they need to offer valid reasons why they think their solution is better than Prudy's. Have them look for evidence in the text that would be likely to convince readers to agree that their idea is better. You may wish to brainstorm a list of persuasive words that students can use in their writing.

Students' paragraphs should:

- offer their idea for a better solution to Prudy's problem
- support their claim with valid reasons
- use linking words and phrases, such as *because* and *for example,* to connect their claim and reasons
- demonstrate strong command of the conventions of standard written English

---

© **Common Core State Standards**

Writing 1. Write opinion pieces on topics or texts, supporting a point of view with reasons.

Prudy's Problem and How She Solved It • Unit 2 • Week 3   **47**

Connect the Texts
Argumentative Opinion Piece

Student Prompt Look back at the descriptions of the museums in *Prudy's Problem and How She Solved It* and "Meeting the Challenge of Collecting." Which museum do you think would be more interesting to visit? Why? State your opinion. Provide supporting evidence from both texts.

_____

_____

_____

_____

_____

_____

_____

_____

_____

_____

_____

_____

_____

_____

_____

_____

_____

_____

Connect the Texts
Argumentative Opinion Piece

Student Prompt, p. 48 Look back at the descriptions of the museums in *Prudy's Problem and How She Solved It* and "Meeting the Challenge of Collecting." Which museum do you think would be more interesting to visit? Why? State your opinion. Provide supporting evidence from both texts.

Writing to Sources Discuss students' opinions and why they formed those opinions. Have them go back into both texts and find specific evidence to support their opinion. Point out that they will also need to consider what they know about themselves and other people, keeping in mind that while these details can be useful support, they are not as valid as evidence from the texts.

	4-point Argument Writing Rubric				
Score	Statement of Purpose/Focus	Organization	Development of Evidence	Language and Vocabulary	Conventions
4	Opinion is clearly conveyed and well supported; response is focused.	Organization is clear and effective, creating a sense of cohesion.	Evidence is thorough and persuasive and includes facts and details.	Ideas are clearly and effectively conveyed, using precise language and/or domain-specific vocabulary.	Command of conventions is strongly demonstrated.
3	Opinion is clear, adequately supported; response is generally focused.	Organization is clear, though minor flaws may be present and some ideas may be disconnected.	Evidence is adequate and includes facts and details.	Ideas are adequately conveyed, using both precise and more general language; may include domain-specific vocabulary.	Command of conventions is sufficiently demonstrated.
2	Opinion is somewhat supported; response may lack focus or include unnecessary material.	Organization is inconsistent, and flaws are apparent.	Evidence is uneven or incomplete; insufficient use of facts and details.	Ideas are unevenly conveyed, using overly-simplistic language; lack of domain-specific vocabulary.	Command of conventions is uneven.
1	The response may be confusing, unfocused; opinion not sufficiently supported.	Organization is poor or nonexistent.	Evidence is poor or nonexistent.	Ideas are conveyed in a vague, unclear, or confusing manner.	There is very little command of conventions.
0	The response shows no evidence of the ability to construct a coherent opinion essay using information from sources.				

ⓒ Common Core State Standards

Writing 1. Write opinion pieces on topics or texts, supporting a point of view with reasons.

Write Like a Reporter
Argumentative Paragraph

Student Prompt Reread pp. 316–317, 320, and 322–323 of *Tops & Bottoms*. Do you think what Hare and his family did in the story is fair? Write an opinion piece in which you state and defend your opinion. Provide evidence from the text and your inferences about the text to support your opinion.

_____

_____

_____

_____

_____

_____

_____

_____

_____

_____

_____

_____

_____

_____

_____

_____

_____

_____

_____

_____

Write Like a Reporter
Argumentative Paragraph

> **Student Prompt, p. 50** Reread pp. 316–317, 320, and 322–323 of *Tops & Bottoms.* Do you think what Hare and his family did in the story is fair? Write an opinion piece in which you state and defend your opinion. Provide evidence from the text and your inferences about the text to support your opinion.

Writing to Sources Encourage students to review the entire story, first focusing on Bear's and the Hare family's situations at the beginning of the story before moving on to the actions of the Hare family and Bear. Have students decide whether they stand with the Hare family or with Bear and write their opinion. Then have them use evidence in the text and their inferences from the text to support their opinion.

Students' paragraphs should:
- state their opinion on the topic clearly
- provide evidence and inferences that support their opinion
- create an effective organizational structure
- demonstrate strong command of the conventions of standard written English

Ⓒ **Common Core State Standards**

Writing 1. Write opinion pieces on topics or texts, supporting a point of view with reasons.

Connect the Texts
Argumentative Opinion Piece

Student Prompt *Tops & Bottoms* and "The Hare and the Tortoise" are both stories that teach a lesson. Which lesson do you think is more valuable—"Be careful what you agree to in a deal" or "Slow and steady wins the race"? Review the stories and draw a conclusion based on details in the texts and your inferences from the texts. Write your opinion. Provide evidence from both texts to support your opinion.

_____

_____

_____

_____

_____

_____

_____

_____

_____

_____

_____

_____

_____

_____

Connect the Texts
Argumentative Opinion Piece

Student Prompt, p. 52 *Tops & Bottoms* and "The Hare and the Tortoise" are both stories that teach a lesson. Which lesson do you think is more valuable— "Be careful what you agree to in a deal" or "Slow and steady wins the race"? Review the stories and draw a conclusion based on details in the texts and your inferences from the texts. Write your opinion. Provide evidence from both texts to support your opinion.

Writing to Sources Ask students to tell their conclusions and to explain why they drew those conclusions. Have them return to both texts to look for evidence to support their opinion. Remind students to look closely at the authors' words and phrases and to think about the inferences readers can make from this language.

		4-point Argument Writing Rubric			
Score	**Statement of Purpose/Focus**	**Organization**	**Development of Evidence**	**Language and Vocabulary**	**Conventions**
4	Opinion is clearly conveyed and well supported; response is focused.	Organization is clear and effective, creating a sense of cohesion.	Evidence is thorough and persuasive and includes facts and details.	Ideas are clearly and effectively conveyed, using precise language and/or domain-specific vocabulary.	Command of conventions is strongly demonstrated.
3	Opinion is clear, adequately supported; response is generally focused.	Organization is clear, though minor flaws may be present and some ideas may be disconnected.	Evidence is adequate and includes facts and details.	Ideas are adequately conveyed, using both precise and more general language; may include domain-specific vocabulary.	Command of conventions is sufficiently demonstrated.
2	Opinion is somewhat supported; response may lack focus or include unnecessary material.	Organization is inconsistent, and flaws are apparent.	Evidence is uneven or incomplete; insufficient use of facts and details.	Ideas are unevenly conveyed, using overly-simplistic language; lack of domain-specific vocabulary.	Command of conventions is uneven.
1	The response may be confusing, unfocused; opinion not sufficiently supported.	Organization is poor or nonexistent.	Evidence is poor or nonexistent.	Ideas are conveyed in a vague, unclear, or confusing manner.	There is very little command of conventions.
0	The response shows no evidence of the ability to construct a coherent opinion essay using information from sources.				

Ⓒ Common Core State Standards

Writing 1. Write opinion pieces on topics or texts, supporting a point of view with reasons.

Write Like a Reporter
Argumentative Paragraph

Student Prompt Reread the selection *Amazing Bird Nests*. Which bird nest do you think is most amazing? Why? Write your opinion. Then provide facts and details from the text as evidence to support your opinion. Finally, write a concluding statement that sums up your ideas.

_____

_____

_____

_____

_____

_____

_____

_____

_____

_____

_____

_____

_____

_____

_____

_____

_____

_____

Write Like a Reporter
Argumentative Paragraph

> **Student Prompt, p. 54** Reread the selection *Amazing Bird Nests.* Which bird nest do you think is most amazing? Why? Write your opinion. Then provide facts and details from the text as evidence to support your opinion. Finally, write a concluding statement that sums up your ideas.

Writing to Sources Point out to students that they will need to reread the text carefully, looking for specific words and sentences they can use as evidence to support their opinion. Tell them to first state their opinion clearly and then to provide two or three reasons supported by facts and details.

Students' paragraphs should:

- state a clear opinion about the topic
- use appropriate text evidence to support their opinion
- provide a concluding statement
- demonstrate strong command of the conventions of standard written English

© Common Core State Standards

Writing 1. Write opinion pieces on topics or texts, supporting a point of view with reasons.

Connect the Texts
Argumentative Opinion Piece

Student Prompt Which do you think would make a more appealing television show—the facts about amazing bird nests or the story of Half-Chicken? Write your opinion. Use details from the texts not only to support the selection you chose but also to explain why you did not choose the other selection. Include persuasive words to convince readers to agree with your choice.

_____

_____

_____

_____

_____

_____

_____

_____

_____

_____

_____

_____

_____

_____

_____

Connect the Texts
Argumentative Opinion Piece

Student Prompt, p. 56 Which do you think would make a more appealing television show—the facts about amazing bird nests or the story of Half-Chicken? Write your opinion. Use details from the texts not only to support the selection you chose but also to explain why you did not choose the other selection. Include persuasive words to convince readers to agree with your choice.

Writing to Sources Suggest that students review the texts and make lists of reasons why each would or would not make a good television show. They can use the lists first to help them form their opinion and then to support that opinion with evidence from both texts. Encourage students to include persuasive words, such as *must, better, entertaining,* and *educational,* that will appeal to readers.

	4-point Argument Writing Rubric				
Score	**Statement of Purpose/Focus**	**Organization**	**Development of Evidence**	**Language and Vocabulary**	**Conventions**
4	Opinion is clearly conveyed and well supported; response is focused.	Organization is clear and effective, creating a sense of cohesion.	Evidence is thorough and persuasive and includes facts and details.	Ideas are clearly and effectively conveyed, using precise language and/or domain-specific vocabulary.	Command of conventions is strongly demonstrated.
3	Opinion is clear, adequately supported; response is generally focused.	Organization is clear, though minor flaws may be present and some ideas may be disconnected.	Evidence is adequate and includes facts and details.	Ideas are adequately conveyed, using both precise and more general language; may include domain-specific vocabulary.	Command of conventions is sufficiently demonstrated.
2	Opinion is somewhat supported; response may lack focus or include unnecessary material.	Organization is inconsistent, and flaws are apparent.	Evidence is uneven or incomplete; insufficient use of facts and details.	Ideas are unevenly conveyed, using overly-simplistic language; lack of domain-specific vocabulary.	Command of conventions is uneven.
1	The response may be confusing, unfocused; opinion not sufficiently supported.	Organization is poor or nonexistent.	Evidence is poor or nonexistent.	Ideas are conveyed in a vague, unclear, or confusing manner.	There is very little command of conventions.
0	The response shows no evidence of the ability to construct a coherent opinion essay using information from sources.				

Ⓒ Common Core State Standards

Writing 1. Write opinion pieces on topics or texts, supporting a point of view with reasons.

Prove It!
Argumentative Review

Making a Choice

Argumentative Review

In this unit, students have read examples of argumentative writing, including an advertisement, and have had the opportunity to write in this mode. Remind students of texts and writing tasks (such as Write Like a Reporter and Connect the Texts) in which they have encountered and practiced argumentative writing.

Key Features of an Argumentative Review

- states the writer's opinion of a story, book, movie, play, television show, etc.
- supports the opinion with reasons backed by facts and details from the source
- uses an organizational structure that lists the reasons in a logical order
- uses persuasive words such as *best, important,* and *should* to try to convince readers to agree with the opinion
- uses linking words and phrases such as *because* and *for example* to connect the opinion and the reasons
- provides a concluding statement that usually summarizes the writer's main point

Writing Task Overview

Each unit writing task provides students with an opportunity to write to sources. To successfully complete the task, students must analyze, synthesize, and evaluate multiple complex texts and create their own written response.

Making a Choice

Part 1: Students will read and take notes on the selected sources. They will then respond to several questions about these sources and discuss their written responses with partners or in small groups.

Part 2: Students will work individually to plan, write, and revise their own argumentative reviews.

Scorable Products: evidence-based short responses, argumentative review

Making a Choice: Writing Task – Short Response

Teacher Directions:

1. Introduce the Sources Refer students to the following texts in the Student Edition:

1. *I Wanna Iguana,* pp. 240–255

2. *Prudy's Problem and How She Solved It,* pp. 274–289

3. *Tops & Bottoms,* pp. 308–325

Explain to students that they will need to draw evidence and support from the texts above in order to answer evidence-based short response questions and to write a review. Students should take notes and categorize information as they closely reread the texts. Students should be given paper or a relevant graphic organizer from the TR DVD for note-taking.

2. Provide Student Directions and Scoring Information (p. 62) Answer any task-related questions students may have. If necessary, provide additional paper for students to write their responses.

3. Initiate the Writing Task If you are timing this part of the task, you may wish to alert students when half the allotted time has elapsed and again when 5 minutes remain.

4. Facilitate Collaboration After students have completed their written responses to the evidence-based short response questions, assign partners or small groups and have them discuss their responses. If students struggle to work together productively, provide them with tips and strategies for expressing their ideas and building on others'.

Ⓒ **Common Core State Standards**

Writing 1. Write opinion pieces on topics or texts, supporting a point of view with reasons. **Writing 1.a.** Introduce the topic or text they are writing about, state an opinion, and create an organizational structure that lists reasons. **Writing 1.b.** Provide reasons that support the opinion. **Writing 1.c.** Use linking words and phrases (e.g., *because, therefore, since, for example*) to connect opinion and reasons. **Writing 1.d.** Provide a concluding statement or section.

Scoring Information

Use the following 2-point scoring rubrics to evaluate students' answers to the evidence-based short response questions.

1. Look closely at the characters, settings, plots, and themes in the three stories. How do these story elements play a role in your feelings about each story?

Analysis Rubric	
2	The response: • demonstrates the ability to analyze story elements across texts • includes specific details that make reference to the texts
1	The response: • demonstrates a limited ability to analyze story elements across texts • includes some details that make reference to the texts
0	A response receives no credit if it demonstrates no ability to analyze story elements across texts or includes no relevant details from the texts.

2. What do you think makes a good story? Cite examples from the texts that show how strong story elements contribute to a good story.

Synthesis Rubric	
2	The response: • demonstrates the ability to synthesize information from the sources in order to describe the characteristics of a good story • includes specific details that make reference to the texts
1	The response: • demonstrates a limited ability to synthesize information from the sources in order to describe the characteristics of a good story • includes some details that make reference to the texts
0	A response receives no credit if it demonstrates no ability to synthesize information from the sources or includes no relevant details from the texts.

3. Prepare a list of questions you can use to evaluate a story and form an opinion about it. Rate each selection using your questions. Cite examples from the texts.

	Evaluation Rubric
2	The response: • demonstrates the ability to evaluate texts in order to create a list of questions to form an opinion about the texts • includes specific details that make reference to the texts
1	The response: • demonstrates a limited ability to evaluate texts in order to create a list of questions to form an opinion about the texts • includes some details that make reference to the texts
0	A response receives no credit if it demonstrates no ability to evaluate texts or includes no relevant details from the texts.

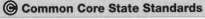

Common Core State Standards

Writing 1. Write opinion pieces on topics or texts, supporting a point of view with reasons. **Writing 1.a.** Introduce the topic or text they are writing about, state an opinion, and create an organizational structure that lists reasons. **Writing 1.b.** Provide reasons that support the opinion. **Writing 1.c.** Use linking words and phrases (e.g., *because*, *therefore*, *since*, *for example*) to connect opinion and reasons. **Writing 1.d.** Provide a concluding statement or section.

Making a Choice
Writing Task – Short Response

Student Directions:

Your Assignment You will reread several selections from Unit 2 and take notes on these sources. Then you will answer three questions about these texts. You may refer to your notes or to any of the sources as often as you like.

Sources

1. *I Wanna Iguana,* pp. 240–255

2. *Prudy's Problem and How She Solved It,* pp. 274–289

3. *Tops & Bottoms,* pp. 308–325

Be sure to read closely and take good notes. Your sources and notes will be the basis for writing your own review in the second half of this writing task.

Evidence-Based Short Response Questions Answer the short response questions on the lines provided below each question. Your answers to these questions will be scored. Be sure to base your answers on the sources you have just read. Remember that you may refer back to your notes or to any of the sources.

After you have answered the questions, you will discuss your responses with a partner or within a small group. Your teacher will let you know when to begin the discussion part of this task.

Scoring Information Your responses will be scored based on evidence of your ability to:

- compare information across texts
- include specific details that are clearly drawn from the sources
- locate and select information from the sources
- identify important information

Evidence-Based Short Response Questions

1. Look closely at the characters, settings, plots, and themes in the three stories. How do these story elements play a role in your feelings about each story?

_____

_____

_____

_____

2. What do you think makes a good story? Cite examples from the texts that show how strong story elements contribute to a good story.

_____

_____

_____

_____

3. Prepare a list of questions you can use to evaluate a story and form an opinion about it. Rate each selection using your questions. Cite examples from the texts.

_____

_____

_____

_____

Collaborative Discussion

After you have written your responses to the questions, discuss your ideas. Your teacher will assign you a partner or a small group and let you know when to begin.

Making a Choice: Writing Task – Review

Teacher Directions:

1. **Provide Student Directions and Scoring Information (p. 66)** Explain to students that they will now review their notes and sources and plan, draft, and revise their argumentative reviews. Although they may use their notes and sources, they must work alone. Students will be allowed to look back at the answers they wrote to the short response questions, but they are not allowed to make changes to those answers. Have students read the directions for the review and answer any task-related questions they may have. Students should be given paper on which to write their reviews.

2. **Initiate the Writing Task** If you are timing this part of the task, you may wish to suggest approximate times for students to begin writing and revising. If students wish to continue writing rather than revising, allow them to do so. Alert students when 5 minutes remain.

3. **Scoring Information** Use the scoring rubric on the next page to evaluate students' reviews.

4. **Review Prompt** Reread *I Wanna Iguana, Prudy's Problem and How She Solved It,* and *Tops & Bottoms*. Write a review of the selection you think is the best story of the three. State your opinion and support it with reasons. Use examples from all three texts to defend your choice.

	4-point Argument Writing Rubric				
Score	**Statement of Purpose/Focus**	**Organization**	**Development of Evidence**	**Language and Vocabulary**	**Conventions**
4	Review clearly conveys and supports opinion of literature.	Organization includes a clear opinion, strong reasons, and a concluding statement.	Evidence includes sufficient facts and details from sources.	Persuasive and linking words are effectively used to enhance and connect ideas.	Command of conventions is clearly demonstrated.
3	Review adequately conveys and supports opinion of literature.	Organization includes an opinion, reasons, and a concluding statement.	Evidence includes some facts and details from sources.	Persuasive and linking words are used to enhance and connect ideas.	Command of conventions is sufficient.
2	Review somewhat supports opinion; includes unnecessary details.	Organization lacks an opinion or conclusion; reasons are unclear.	Evidence does not include facts and details from sources.	Few persuasive and linking words are used.	Command of conventions is uneven.
1	Review is confusing; opinion is not supported.	Organization lacks opinion, reasons, and conclusion.	Evidence is poor or nonexistent.	There is little or no use of persuasive or linking words.	There is very little correct use of conventions.
0	The response shows no evidence of the ability to construct a coherent review using information from sources.				

ⓒ Common Core State Standards

Writing 1. Write opinion pieces on topics or texts, supporting a point of view with reasons. **Writing 1.a.** Introduce the topic or text they are writing about, state an opinion, and create an organizational structure that lists reasons. **Writing 1.b.** Provide reasons that support the opinion. **Writing 1.c.** Use linking words and phrases (e.g., *because*, *therefore*, *since*, *for example*) to connect opinion and reasons. **Writing 1.d.** Provide a concluding statement or section.

Making a Choice:
Writing Task – Review

Student Directions:

Your Assignment Now you will use your notes and sources to plan, draft, and revise your review. While you may use your notes and refer to your sources, you must work on your own. You may also refer to the answers you wrote to earlier questions, but you cannot change those answers.

Review Prompt Reread *I Wanna Iguana, Prudy's Problem and How She Solved It,* and *Tops & Bottoms*. Write a review of the selection you think is the best story of the three. State your opinion and support it with reasons. Use examples from all three texts to defend your choice.

Scoring Information Your review will be assigned a score for

1. **Focus** – how well you maintain your focus and convey your ideas clearly

2. **Organization** – how well your ideas flow from introduction to opinions and reasons to concluding statement

3. **Development** – how well you use details from the texts to support your opinion

4. **Language and Vocabulary** – how well you use linking words and phrases to connect your opinion and reasons

5. **Conventions** – how well you follow the rules of usage, punctuation, capitalization, and spelling

Now begin work on your review. Try to manage your time carefully so that you can

- plan your review
- write your review
- revise and edit for a final draft

Making a Choice: Writing Task – Review

Teacher Directions:

1. Publish Explain to students that publishing their writing is the last step in the writing process. If time permits, have students look at one another's compositions and incorporate any comment their classmates have. Discuss different ways technology can be used to publish writing.

2. Present Students will now have the option to present their reviews. Have students read aloud their reviews to the class. Use the list below to offer students tips on listening and speaking.

While Listening to a Classmate...

- Listen carefully.
- Think of relevant questions.

While Speaking to Classmates...

- Speak clearly at an appropriate pace.
- Face the audience.

Things to Do Together...

- Build on others' ideas.
- Ask questions to check understanding.

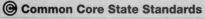

Common Core State Standards

Writing 1. Write opinion pieces on topics or texts, supporting a point of view with reasons. **Writing 1.a.** Introduce the topic or text they are writing about, state an opinion, and create an organizational structure that lists reasons. **Writing 1.b.** Provide reasons that support the opinion. **Writing 1.c.** Use linking words and phrases (e.g., *because*, *therefore*, *since*, *for example*) to connect opinion and reasons. **Writing 1.d.** Provide a concluding statement or section.

Unit 3 People and Nature

Writing Focus: Informative/Explanatory

Write Like a Reporter
Informative/Explanatory Paragraph

Student Prompt Reread pp. 383–390 of *How Do You Raise a Raisin?* Think about how raisins are made. Write an explanation of the process as a series of steps. Use information from the text to tell what is involved in each step. Add time-order words to clarify the sequence of the steps.

_____

_____

_____

_____

_____

_____

_____

_____

_____

_____

_____

_____

_____

_____

_____

_____

Write Like a Reporter
Informative/Explanatory Paragraph

Student Prompt, p. 70 Reread pp. 383–390 of *How Do You Raise a Raisin?*
Think about how raisins are made. Write an explanation of the process as a
series of steps. Use information from the text to tell what is involved in each
step. Add time-order words to clarify the sequence of the steps.

Writing to Sources Tell students to state their topic at the beginning of their
explanation. Remind them that they will need to look in the text for facts and details
about making raisins. Brainstorm a list of time-order words, such as *first, next, later,*
and *after,* for students to use in their explanation.

Students' explanations should:
- introduce the topic
- develop the topic supported by facts and details from the text
- use time-order words to indicate the order of the steps in the process
- demonstrate strong command of the conventions of standard written English

Writing 2. Write informative/explanatory texts to examine a topic and convey ideas and information clearly.

Connect the Texts
Informative/Explanatory Paragraph

Student Prompt Compare and contrast *How Do You Raise a Raisin?* and "Worms at Work." Look at their organization and graphics as well as their words. Write an explanation of how the texts are alike and how they are different. Provide evidence from the texts to support your ideas.

_____

_____

_____

_____

_____

_____

_____

_____

_____

_____

_____

_____

_____

_____

_____

_____

Connect the Texts
Informative/Explanatory Paragraph

Student Prompt, p. 72 Compare and contrast *How Do You Raise a Raisin?* and "Worms at Work." Look at their organization and graphics as well as their words. Write an explanation of how the texts are alike and how they are different. Provide evidence from the texts to support your ideas.

Writing to Sources Ask students to go back into the texts and find similarities and differences to list on a two-column chart. Suggest that students begin by identifying the genre of each text. Explain that a chart of evidence drawn from the texts will help them organize their ideas before they write their explanation.

Informative/Explanatory Writing Rubric					
Score	Focus	Organization	Development of Evidence	Language and Vocabulary	Conventions
4	Main idea is clearly conveyed and well supported; response is focused.	Organization is clear and effective, creating a sense of cohesion.	Evidence is relevant and thorough; includes facts and details.	Ideas are clearly and effectively conveyed, using precise language and/or domain-specific vocabulary.	Command of conventions is strongly demonstrated.
3	Main idea is clear, adequately supported; response is generally focused.	Organization is clear, though minor flaws may be present and some ideas may be disconnected.	Evidence is adequate and includes facts and details.	Ideas are adequately conveyed, using both precise and more general language; may include domain-specific vocabulary.	Command of conventions is sufficiently demonstrated.
2	Main idea is somewhat supported; lacks focus or includes unnecessary material.	Organization is inconsistent, and flaws are apparent.	Evidence is uneven or incomplete; insufficient use of facts and details.	Ideas are unevenly conveyed, using overly-simplistic language; lacks domain-specific vocabulary.	Command of conventions is uneven.
1	Response may be confusing, unfocused; main idea insufficiently supported.	Organization is poor or nonexistent.	Evidence is poor or nonexistent.	Ideas are conveyed in a vague, unclear, or confusing manner.	There is very little command of conventions.
0	The response shows no evidence of the ability to construct a coherent explanatory essay using information from sources.				

Ⓒ Common Core State Standards

Writing 2. Write informative/explanatory texts to examine a topic and convey ideas and information clearly.

Write Like a Reporter
Informative/Explanatory Paragraph

Student Prompt Reread pp. 421–423 of *Pushing Up the Sky*. Write a summary describing what the characters in the play are trying to do and how they try to do it. Include an explanation of what the myth demonstrates about cooperation. How does cooperation figure into the story's resolution? Use text details to support your ideas.

_____

_____

_____

_____

_____

_____

_____

_____

_____

_____

_____

_____

_____

_____

_____

_____

_____

_____

Write Like a Reporter
Informative/Explanatory Paragraph

Student Prompt, p. 74 Reread pp. 421–423 of *Pushing Up the Sky*. Write a summary describing what the characters in the play are trying to do and how they try to do it. Include an explanation of what the myth demonstrates about cooperation. How does cooperation figure into the story's resolution? Use text details to support your ideas.

Writing to Sources Remind students that writing a summary involves using their own words to tell the most important ideas or events of a selection in a few sentences. Their summary should focus on the events on pp. 421–423. Students should explain what these story events reveal about cooperation: that the problem isn't solved until everyone works together. Have students provide text evidence to support their ideas.

Students' explanations should:

- include a summary of the major events in part of the story
- tell what those events reveal about the given topic
- provide facts and details from the text to support their ideas
- demonstrate strong command of the conventions of standard written English

© **Common Core State Standards**

Writing 2. Write informative/explanatory texts to examine a topic and convey ideas and information clearly.

Pushing Up the Sky • Unit 3 • Week 2   **75**

Connect the Texts

Informative/Explanatory Comparison

Student Prompt Look back at *Pushing Up the Sky* and "Catch It and Run!" Compare and contrast these two myths. Describe their characters, settings, plots, and themes. Write an explanation of how the texts are alike and different. Support your ideas with evidence from both texts.

_____

_____

_____

_____

_____

_____

_____

_____

_____

_____

_____

_____

_____

_____

_____

_____

Connect the Texts
Informative/Explanatory Comparison

> **Student Prompt, p. 76** Look back at *Pushing Up the Sky* and "Catch It and Run!" Compare and contrast these two myths. Describe their characters, settings, plots, and themes. Write an explanation of how the texts are alike and different. Support your ideas with evidence from both texts.

Writing to Sources Have students return to the texts and find and write similarities and differences on a Venn diagram. Point out that since both texts are myths, students can write this detail in the center section of the diagram. When they have finished filling in their diagram, tell students that as they write, they can use this evidence from the texts to help them organize and support their ideas.

	Informative/Explanatory Writing Rubric				
Score	**Focus**	**Organization**	**Development of Evidence**	**Language and Vocabulary**	**Conventions**
4	Main idea is clearly conveyed and well supported; response is focused.	Organization is clear and effective, creating a sense of cohesion.	Evidence is relevant and thorough; includes facts and details.	Ideas are clearly and effectively conveyed, using precise language and/or domain-specific vocabulary.	Command of conventions is strongly demonstrated.
3	Main idea is clear, adequately supported; response is generally focused.	Organization is clear, though minor flaws may be present and some ideas may be disconnected.	Evidence is adequate and includes facts and details.	Ideas are adequately conveyed, using both precise and more general language; may include domain-specific vocabulary.	Command of conventions is sufficiently demonstrated.
2	Main idea is somewhat supported; lacks focus or includes unnecessary material.	Organization is inconsistent, and flaws are apparent.	Evidence is uneven or incomplete; insufficient use of facts and details.	Ideas are unevenly conveyed, using overly-simplistic language; lacks domain-specific vocabulary.	Command of conventions is uneven.
1	Response may be confusing, unfocused; main idea insufficiently supported.	Organization is poor or nonexistent.	Evidence is poor or nonexistent.	Ideas are conveyed in a vague, unclear, or confusing manner.	There is very little command of conventions.
0	The response shows no evidence of the ability to construct a coherent explanatory essay using information from sources.				

©ⓒ Common Core State Standards

Writing 2. Write informative/explanatory texts to examine a topic and convey ideas and information clearly.

Write Like a Reporter
Informative/Explanatory Paragraph

Student Prompt Reread pp. 449–451 of *Seeing Stars*. Look for and list details from the text that answer this question: How can you see stars at night? Write a short report on the topic using the facts from the text. Introduce the topic at the beginning and provide a concluding statement.

_____

_____

_____

_____

_____

_____

_____

_____

_____

_____

_____

_____

_____

_____

_____

_____

Write Like a Reporter

Informative/Explanatory Paragraph

Student Prompt, p. 78 Reread pp. 449–451 of *Seeing Stars*. Look for and list details from the text that answer this question: How can you see stars at night? Write a short report on the topic using the facts from the text. Introduce the topic at the beginning and provide a concluding statement.

Writing to Sources Have students write the question and then look closely at the given pages to find and write information that specifically answers the question. Explain that they will need to organize the information in a way that makes sense, grouping related ideas and using linking words and phrases. Remind students to provide introductory and concluding statements in their report.

Students' reports should:

- introduce the topic and group related information together
- connect ideas using linking words and phrases such as *also, and,* and *but*
- provide a concluding statement
- demonstrate strong command of the conventions of standard written English

© Common Core State Standards

Writing 2. Write informative/explanatory texts to examine a topic and convey ideas and information clearly.

Connect the Texts
Informative/Explanatory Report

Student Prompt Think about the authors and their selections *Seeing Stars* and "Scien-Trickery: Riddles in Science." Write a short report that focuses on the authors' topics, genres, use of language, and purposes for writing. Use evidence from the texts to support your ideas.

_____

_____

_____

_____

_____

_____

_____

_____

_____

_____

_____

_____

_____

_____

_____

_____

_____

_____

Connect the Texts

Informative/Explanatory Report

Student Prompt, p. 80 Think about the authors and their selections *Seeing Stars* and "Scien-Trickery: Riddles in Science." Write a short report that focuses on the authors' topics, genres, use of language, and purposes for writing. Use evidence from the texts to support your ideas.

Writing to Sources Have students review both texts. Suggest that they make and fill in a chart with two columns for the authors and their selections and four rows for the listed categories. Point out that this chart will help students gather details from the texts and organize their ideas before they begin writing.

	Informative/Explanatory Writing Rubric				
Score	**Focus**	**Organization**	**Development of Evidence**	**Language and Vocabulary**	**Conventions**
4	Main idea is clearly conveyed and well supported; response is focused.	Organization is clear and effective, creating a sense of cohesion.	Evidence is relevant and thorough; includes facts and details.	Ideas are clearly and effectively conveyed, using precise language and/or domain-specific vocabulary.	Command of conventions is strongly demonstrated.
3	Main idea is clear, adequately supported; response is generally focused.	Organization is clear, though minor flaws may be present and some ideas may be disconnected.	Evidence is adequate and includes facts and details.	Ideas are adequately conveyed, using both precise and more general language; may include domain-specific vocabulary.	Command of conventions is sufficiently demonstrated.
2	Main idea is somewhat supported; lacks focus or includes unnecessary material.	Organization is inconsistent, and flaws are apparent.	Evidence is uneven or incomplete; insufficient use of facts and details.	Ideas are unevenly conveyed, using overly-simplistic language; lacks domain-specific vocabulary.	Command of conventions is uneven.
1	Response may be confusing, unfocused; main idea insufficiently supported.	Organization is poor or nonexistent.	Evidence is poor or nonexistent.	Ideas are conveyed in a vague, unclear, or confusing manner.	There is very little command of conventions.
0	The response shows no evidence of the ability to construct a coherent explanatory essay using information from sources.				

© **Common Core State Standards**

Writing 2. Write informative/explanatory texts to examine a topic and convey ideas and information clearly.

Write Like a Reporter
Informative/Explanatory Paragraph

Student Prompt Reread *A Symphony of Whales*. Look for facts in the text and illustrations about the lives of the villagers in the Arctic. Use these facts to write a short report about aspects of their lives such as food, clothing, houses, transportation, and beliefs.

_____

_____

_____

_____

_____

_____

_____

_____

_____

_____

_____

_____

_____

_____

Write Like a Reporter
Informative/Explanatory Paragraph

Student Prompt, p. 82 Reread *A Symphony of Whales*. Look for facts in the text and illustrations about the lives of the villagers in the Arctic. Use these facts to write a short report about aspects of their lives such as food, clothing, houses, transportation, and beliefs.

Writing to Sources As students reread the selection, have them take notes on the facts they find about the villagers' lives. Suggest that students organize these notes by category and then arrange the categories in a logical order. Point out that this preparation will help them when they write their report.

Students' reports should:

- state the topic clearly
- group related information by category
- use facts and details from the text
- demonstrate strong command of the conventions of standard written English

Ⓒ **Common Core State Standards**

Writing 2. Write informative/explanatory texts to examine a topic and convey ideas and information clearly.

A Symphony of Whales • Unit 3 • Week 4 **83**

Name _____

Connect the Texts
Informative/Explanatory Report

Student Prompt Look back at *A Symphony of Whales* and "He Listens to Whales." Both selections contain information about whale songs. Find this information and use it to write a short report on whale songs. Organize your report using the text structure of main idea and details.

_____

_____

_____

_____

_____

_____

_____

_____

_____

_____

_____

_____

_____

_____

_____

_____

_____

Connect the Texts
Informative/Explanatory Report

Student Prompt, p. 84 Look back at *A Symphony of Whales* and "He Listens to Whales." Both selections contain information about whale songs. Find this information and use it to write a short report on whale songs. Organize your report using the text structure of main idea and details.

Writing to Sources Tell students to read the fictional story carefully to find several facts about whale songs. In the magazine article, the last section, "Long Songs," is about whale songs. Students may want to take notes on both selections first and then organize the facts they find. Have students consider what idea all the facts relate to as a way of identifying a main idea.

\\ Informative/Explanatory Writing Rubric					
Score	**Focus**	**Organization**	**Development of Evidence**	**Language and Vocabulary**	**Conventions**
4	Main idea is clearly conveyed and well supported; response is focused.	Organization is clear and effective, creating a sense of cohesion.	Evidence is relevant and thorough; includes facts and details.	Ideas are clearly and effectively conveyed, using precise language and/or domain-specific vocabulary.	Command of conventions is strongly demonstrated.
3	Main idea is clear, adequately supported; response is generally focused.	Organization is clear, though minor flaws may be present and some ideas may be disconnected.	Evidence is adequate and includes facts and details.	Ideas are adequately conveyed, using both precise and more general language; may include domain-specific vocabulary.	Command of conventions is sufficiently demonstrated.
2	Main idea is somewhat supported; lacks focus or includes unnecessary material.	Organization is inconsistent, and flaws are apparent.	Evidence is uneven or incomplete; insufficient use of facts and details.	Ideas are unevenly conveyed, using overly-simplistic language; lacks domain-specific vocabulary.	Command of conventions is uneven.
1	Response may be confusing, unfocused; main idea insufficiently supported.	Organization is poor or nonexistent.	Evidence is poor or nonexistent.	Ideas are conveyed in a vague, unclear, or confusing manner.	There is very little command of conventions.
0	The response shows no evidence of the ability to construct a coherent explanatory essay using information from sources.				

Ⓒ **Common Core State Standards**

Writing 2. Write informative/explanatory texts to examine a topic and convey ideas and information clearly.

Write Like a Reporter
Informative/Explanatory Paragraph

Student Prompt Which two animals in *Around One Cactus* are dangerous to people? Use information from the poem and the Field Notes to identify these animals and what makes them dangerous. Then write an explanation describing what these two animals do that makes them a danger to people.

_____

_____

_____

_____

_____

_____

_____

_____

_____

_____

_____

_____

_____

_____

_____

_____

Write Like a Reporter

Informative/Explanatory Paragraph

Student Prompt, p. 86 Which two animals in *Around One Cactus* are dangerous to people? Use information from the poem and the Field Notes to identify these animals and what makes them dangerous. Then write an explanation describing what these two animals do that makes them a danger to people.

Writing to Sources Tell students to review the poem to find the two animals that are described with the words *stinging* and *deadly* and then to read about these animals in the Field Notes. Point out that the focus of students' reports is on how these animals are dangerous to people; therefore, the details in their reports should support this main idea. Remind students that these details must come from the text.

Students' reports should:

- state and focus on the main idea
- provide details that support the main idea
- use facts and details from the text
- demonstrate strong command of the conventions of standard written English

Ⓒ **Common Core State Standards**

Writing 2. Write informative/explanatory texts to examine a topic and convey ideas and information clearly.

Around One Cactus • Unit 3 • Week 5   **87**

Connect the Texts
Informative/Explanatory Report

Student Prompt Look back at *Around One Cactus* and "The Water Cycle." Write an explanation of how the water cycle works in the desert environment in *Around One Cactus*. Use facts from both selections to support your explanation.

_____

_____

_____

_____

_____

_____

_____

_____

_____

_____

_____

_____

_____

_____

Connect the Texts
Informative/Explanatory Report

Student Prompt, p. 88 Look back at *Around One Cactus* and "The Water Cycle." Write an explanation of how the water cycle works in the desert environment in *Around One Cactus*. Use facts from both selections to support your explanation.

Writing to Sources Point out that students will need to read both texts closely to identify facts they can use in their explanation and to draw conclusions from those facts. Remind students that graphics often accompany expository text to support or extend information. Suggest that students include diagrams or illustrations with their explanation.

Score	Focus	Organization	Development of Evidence	Language and Vocabulary	Conventions
	Informative/Explanatory Writing Rubric				
4	Main idea is clearly conveyed and well supported; response is focused.	Organization is clear and effective, creating a sense of cohesion.	Evidence is relevant and thorough; includes facts and details.	Ideas are clearly and effectively conveyed, using precise language and/or domain-specific vocabulary.	Command of conventions is strongly demonstrated.
3	Main idea is clear, adequately supported; response is generally focused.	Organization is clear, though minor flaws may be present and some ideas may be disconnected.	Evidence is adequate and includes facts and details.	Ideas are adequately conveyed, using both precise and more general language; may include domain-specific vocabulary.	Command of conventions is sufficiently demonstrated.
2	Main idea is somewhat supported; lacks focus or includes unnecessary material.	Organization is inconsistent, and flaws are apparent.	Evidence is uneven or incomplete; insufficient use of facts and details.	Ideas are unevenly conveyed, using overly-simplistic language; lacks domain-specific vocabulary.	Command of conventions is uneven.
1	Response may be confusing, unfocused; main idea insufficiently supported.	Organization is poor or nonexistent.	Evidence is poor or nonexistent.	Ideas are conveyed in a vague, unclear, or confusing manner.	There is very little command of conventions.
0	The response shows no evidence of the ability to construct a coherent explanatory essay using information from sources.				

© Common Core State Standards

Writing 2. Write informative/explanatory texts to examine a topic and convey ideas and information clearly.

Prove It!
Informative/Explanatory How-to Report

Academic Vocabulary

In a **how-to report,** a writer explains "how to" make or do something. The writer provides a set of steps written in the order in which they are to be followed. These steps may be in a numbered list, or they may be written in paragraphs.

ELL

Introduce Genre Write *how-to* on the board. Explain that this word is used to describe a kind of text that tells about an activity—"how to" make or do something. Point out that a how-to report always has a set of steps. Each step explains how to do one part of the activity. Discuss with students the key features of a how-to report that appear on this page.

Starting a Group Project

Informative/Explanatory How-to Report

In this unit, students have read examples of informative/explanatory writing, including expository text and procedural text, and have had the opportunity to write in this mode. Remind students of texts and writing tasks (such as Write Like a Reporter and Connect the Texts) in which they have encountered and practiced informative/explanatory writing.

Key Features of an Informative/Explanatory How-to Report

- explains the task or activity using a series of steps
- groups related information together
- includes illustrations when useful in aiding comprehension
- develops the topic with facts, definitions, and details
- uses words such as *first, next,* and *last* to show the order of the steps
- uses linking words such as *also, and,* and *but* to connect ideas
- uses sentences with strong verbs to guide readers
- provides a concluding statement

Writing Task Overview

Each unit writing task provides students with an opportunity to write to sources. To successfully complete the task, students must analyze, synthesize, and evaluate multiple complex texts and create their own written responses.

Starting a Group Project

Part 1: Students will read and take notes on the selected sources. They will then respond to several questions about these sources and discuss their written responses with partners or in small groups.

Part 2: Students will work individually to plan, write, and revise their own how-to report.

Scorable Products: evidence-based short responses, how-to report

Starting a Group Project: Writing Task – Short Response

Teacher Directions:

1. Introduce the Sources Refer students to the following texts in the Student Edition:

1. *How Do You Raise a Raisin?,* pp. 378–393

2. *Pushing Up the Sky,* pp. 412–423

3. *A Symphony of Whales,* pp. 476–491

Explain to students that they will need to draw evidence and support from the texts above in order to answer evidence-based short response questions and to write a how-to report. Students should take notes and categorize information as they closely reread the texts. Students should be given paper or a relevant graphic organizer from the TR DVD for note-taking.

2. Provide Student Directions and Scoring Information (p. 94) Answer any task-related questions students may have. If necessary, provide additional paper for students to write their responses.

3. Initiate the Writing Task If you are timing this part of the task, you may wish to alert students when half the allotted time has elapsed and again when 5 minutes remain.

4. Facilitate Collaboration After students have completed their written responses to the evidence-based short response questions, assign partners or small groups and have them discuss their responses. If students struggle to work together productively, provide them with tips and strategies for expressing their ideas and building on others'.

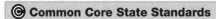

Common Core State Standards

Writing 2. Write informative/explanatory texts to examine a topic and convey ideas and information clearly. **Speaking/Listening 1.** Engage effectively in a range of collaborative discussions (one-on-one, in groups, and teacher-led) with diverse partners on grade 3 topics and texts, building on others' ideas and expressing their own clearly. **(Also Writing 2.a., Writing 2.b., Writing 2.d.)**

Scoring Information

Use the following 2-point scoring rubrics to evaluate students' answers to the evidence-based short response questions.

1. What projects do groups of people work on in the three selections? How are the ways in which the groups work on the projects similar and different?

Analysis Rubric	
2	The response: • demonstrates the ability to analyze and compare details across the texts • includes specific details that make reference to the texts
1	The response: • demonstrates a limited ability to analyze and compare details across the texts • includes some details that make reference to the texts
0	A response receives no credit if it demonstrates no ability to analyze and compare details across the texts or includes no relevant details from the texts.

2. If you were starting a group project, how would you get people interested in the project? Cite examples from the texts of ways people get involved in group projects.

Synthesis Rubric	
2	The response: • demonstrates the ability to synthesize information from the sources in order to describe ways to interest people in a group project • includes specific details that make reference to the texts
1	The response: • demonstrates a limited ability to synthesize information from the sources in order to describe ways to interest people in a group project • includes some details that make reference to the texts
0	A response receives no credit if it demonstrates no ability to synthesize information from the sources or includes no relevant details from the texts.

3. Prepare a checklist to evaluate how well a group of people works on a group project. Rate each group of people in the three selections using this checklist. Cite examples from the text.

Evaluation Rubric	
2	The response: • demonstrates the ability to evaluate texts in order to create a rating checklist and rate groups of people working on group projects • includes specific details that make reference to the texts
1	The response: • demonstrates a limited ability to evaluate texts in order to create a rating checklist and rate groups of people working on group projects • includes some details that make reference to the texts
0	A response receives no credit if it demonstrates no ability to evaluate texts or includes no relevant details from the texts.

© **Common Core State Standards**

Writing 2. Write informative/explanatory texts to examine a topic and convey ideas and information clearly. **Writing 8.** Recall information from experiences or gather information from print and digital sources; take brief notes on sources and sort evidence into provided categories.

Starting a Group Project
Writing Task – Short Response

Student Directions:

Your assignment You will reread several selections from Unit 3 and take notes on these sources. Then you will answer three questions about these materials. You may refer to your notes or to any of the sources as often as you like.

Sources

1. *How Do You Raise a Raisin?,* pp. 378–393

2. *Pushing Up the Sky,* pp. 412–423

3. *A Symphony of Whales,* pp. 476–491

Be sure to read closely and take good notes. Your sources and notes will be the basis for writing your own how-to report in the second half of this writing task.

Evidence-Based Short Response Questions Answer the short response questions on the lines provided below each question. Your answers to these questions will be scored. Be sure to base your answers on the sources you have just read. Remember that you may refer back to your notes or to any of the sources.

After you have answered the questions, you will discuss your responses with a partner or in a small group. Your teacher will let you know when to begin the discussion part of this task.

Scoring Information Your responses will be scored based on how you demonstrate the ability to:

- compare and contrast information across texts
- name ways of getting people interested in a project
- evaluate how well a group works together
- include specific details from the sources

Evidence-Based Short Response Questions

1. What projects do groups of people work on in the three selections? How are the ways in which the groups work on the projects similar and different?

_____

_____

_____

_____

2. If you were starting a group project, how would you get people interested in the project? Give examples from the texts of ways people get involved in group projects.

_____

_____

_____

_____

3. Prepare a checklist to evaluate how well a group of people works on a group project. Rate each group of people in the three selections using this checklist. Cite examples from the text.

_____

_____

_____

_____

Collaborative Discussion

After you have written your responses to the questions, discuss your ideas. Your teacher will assign you a partner or a small group and let you know when to begin.

Starting a Group Project: Writing Task – How-to Report

Teacher Directions:

1. **Provide Student Directions and Scoring Information (p. 98)** Explain to students that they will now review their notes and sources and plan, draft, and revise their how-to reports. Although they may use their notes and sources, they must work alone. Students will be allowed to look back at the answers they wrote to the short response questions, but they are not allowed to make changes to those answers. Have students read the directions for the how-to report and answer any task-related questions they may have. Students should be given paper on which to write their how-to reports.

2. **Initiate the Writing Task** If you are timing this part of the task, you may wish to suggest approximate times for students to begin writing and revising. If students wish to continue writing rather than revising, allow them to do so. Alert students when 5 minutes remain.

3. **Scoring Information** Use the scoring rubric on the next page to evaluate students' how-to reports.

4. **How-to Report Prompt** Review what you learned in *How Do You Raise a Raisin?*, *Pushing Up the Sky*, and *A Symphony of Whales.* Write a how-to report that tells how to start a group project. Explain how to get people involved in the project. Use examples from the selections to support your ideas. Be sure to follow the conventions of written English.

4-point Informative/Explanatory Writing Rubric				
Score	**Focus**	**Organization**	**Development of Evidence**	**Language and Vocabulary**	**Conventions**
4	Main idea is clearly conveyed and well supported; response is focused.	Organization is clear and effective, creating a sense of cohesion.	Evidence is relevant and thorough; includes facts and details.	Ideas are clearly and effectively conveyed, using precise language and/or domain-specific vocabulary.	Command of conventions is strongly demonstrated.
3	Main idea is clear, adequately supported; response is generally focused.	Organization is clear, though minor flaws may be present and some ideas may be disconnected.	Evidence is adequate and includes facts and details.	Ideas are adequately conveyed, using both precise and more general language; may include domain-specific vocabulary.	Command of conventions is sufficiently demonstrated.
2	Main idea is somewhat supported; lacks focus or includes unnecessary material.	Organization is inconsistent, and flaws are apparent.	Evidence is uneven or incomplete; insufficient use of facts or details.	Ideas are unevenly conveyed, using overly-simplistic language; lacks domain-specific vocabulary.	Command of conventions is uneven.
1	Response may be confusing, unfocused; main idea insufficiently supported.	Organization is poor or nonexistent.	Evidence is poor or nonexistent.	Ideas are conveyed in a vague, unclear, or confusing manner.	There is very little command of conventions.
0	The response shows no evidence of the ability to construct a coherent informative/explanatory essay using information from sources.				

© **Common Core State Standards**

Writing 2. Write informative/explanatory texts to examine a topic and convey ideas and information clearly. **Writing 2.a.** Introduce a topic and group related information together; include illustrations when useful to aiding comprehension. **Writing 2.b.** Develop the topic with facts, definitions, and details. **Writing 2.d.** Provide a concluding statement or section.

Starting a Group Project
Writing Task – How-to Report

Student Directions:

Your assignment Now you will review your notes and sources and plan, draft, and revise your how-to report. While you may use your notes and refer to your sources, you must work on your own. You may also refer to the answers you wrote to earlier questions, but you cannot change those answers.

How-to Report Prompt Review what you learned in *How Do You Raise a Raisin?, Pushing Up the Sky,* and *A Symphony of Whales.* Write a how-to report that tells how to start a group project. Explain how to get people involved in the project. Use examples from the selections to support your ideas. Be sure to follow the conventions of written English.

Scoring Information Your how-to report will be assigned a score for

1. **Focus** – how well you maintain your focus and convey ideas and information clearly

2. **Organization** – how well the steps flow logically from first to last using an effective text structure

3. **Development** – how well you develop the topic with facts, definitions, and details

4. **Language and Vocabulary** – how well you use linking words and phrases to connect ideas

5. **Conventions** – how well you follow the rules of usage, punctuation, capitalization, and spelling

Now begin work on your how-to report. Try to manage your time carefully so that you can

- plan your how-to report
- write your how-to report
- revise and edit for a final draft

Starting a Group Project: Writing Task – How-to Report

Teacher Directions:

1. Publish Explain to students that publishing their writing is the last step in the writing process. If time permits, have students review one another's compositions and incorporate any comment their classmates have. Discuss different ways technology can be used to publish writing.

2. Present Students will now have the option to present their how-to reports. Have students give speeches about their how-to reports in front of the class. Use the list below to offer students tips on listening and speaking.

While Listening to a Classmate...

- Think about the speaker is saying.
- Raise your hand to ask a question.

While Speaking to Classmates...

- Stay on topic.
- Speak clearly.

Things to Do Together...

- Follow agreed-upon discussion rules.
- Ask and answer questions.

© Common Core State Standards

Writing 6. With guidance and support from adults, use technology to produce and publish writing (using keyboarding skills) as well as to interact and collaborate with others. **Speaking/Listening 4.** Report on a topic or text, tell a story, or recount an experience with appropriate facts and relevant, descriptive details, speaking clearly at an understandable pace.

Unit 4 One of a Kind

Writing Focus: Narrative

Write Like a Reporter
Narrative Paragraph

Student Prompt Reread p. 36 of *The Man Who Invented Basketball*. Write a story about James and his students the day the first game of basketball was played. Use evidence from the text to help you describe the characters, setting, and events.

_____

_____

_____

_____

_____

_____

_____

_____

_____

_____

_____

_____

_____

_____

_____

_____

_____

Write Like a Reporter
Narrative Paragraph

> **Student Prompt, p. 102** Reread p. 36 of *The Man Who Invented Basketball*. Write a story about James and his students the day the first game of basketball was played. Use evidence from the text to help you describe the characters, setting, and events.

Writing to Sources Explain to students that they can use details in a text to visualize the setting and events. Point out that to write a story about the game described in *The Man Who Invented Basketball,* students will need to reread the text carefully, looking for details that will help them visualize the game. Tell students to use their visualizations and the details they find as they write a narrative of the events.

Students' stories should:

- tell about the game described in the selection
- follow a clear and structured sequence of events
- use descriptive details to develop characters and setting
- demonstrate strong command of the conventions of standard written English

Ⓒ **Common Core State Standards**

Writing 3. Write narratives to develop real or imagined experiences or events using effective technique, descriptive details, and clear event sequences.

Connect the Texts
Narrative Story

> **Student Prompt** Look back at *The Man Who Invented Basketball* and "My Turn at Bat." Write a story in which James Naismith and Ted Williams are the main characters. Use evidence from both texts to support the characterizations in your story.

_____

_____

_____

_____

_____

_____

_____

_____

_____

_____

_____

_____

_____

_____

_____

_____

_____

_____

_____

_____

_____

Connect the Texts
Narrative Story

> **Student Prompt, p. 104** Look back at *The Man Who Invented Basketball* and "My Turn at Bat." Write a story in which James Naismith and Ted Williams are the main characters. Use evidence from both texts to support the characterizations in your story.

Writing to Sources Have students make a T-chart with details about James Naismith and Ted Williams. Have them discuss what they know about the characters based on evidence from the texts. Then have students use the chart as they write their story about James and Ted.

			4-point Narrative Writing Rubric		
Score	**Narrative Focus**	**Organization**	**Development of Narrative**	**Language and Vocabulary**	**Conventions**
4	Narrative is clearly focused and developed throughout.	Narrative has a well-developed, logical, easy-to-follow plot.	Narrative includes thorough and effective use of details, dialogue, and description.	Narrative uses precise, concrete sensory language as well as figurative language and/or domain-specific vocabulary.	Narrative has correct grammar, usage, spelling, capitalization, and punctuation.
3	Narrative is mostly focused and developed throughout.	Narrative has a plot, but there may be some lack of clarity and/or unrelated events.	Narrative includes adequate use of details, dialogue and description.	Narrative uses adequate sensory and figurative language and/or domain-specific vocabulary.	Narrative has a few errors but is completely understandable.
2	Narrative is somewhat developed but may occasionally lose focus.	Narrative's plot is difficult to follow, and ideas are not connected well.	Narrative includes only a few details, dialogues, and descriptions.	Language in narrative is not precise or sensory; lacks domain-specific vocabulary.	Narrative has some errors in usage, grammar, spelling and/or punctuation.
1	Narrative may be confusing, unfocused, or too short.	Narrative has little or no apparent plot.	Narrative includes few or no details, dialogue or description.	Language in narrative is vague, unclear, or confusing.	Narrative is hard to follow because of frequent errors.
0	Narrative gets no credit if it does not demonstrate adequate command of narrative writing traits.				

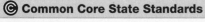

Common Core State Standards

Writing 3. Write narratives to develop real or imagined experiences or events using effective technique, descriptive details, and clear event sequences.

Write Like a Reporter
Narrative Paragraph

Student Prompt Reread pp. 68–69 of *Hottest, Coldest, Highest, Deepest*. Write a tall tale using one of the places described in the text as your setting. Use evidence from the text and the illustrations to support the description of the setting in your story.

_____

_____

_____

_____

_____

_____

_____

_____

_____

_____

_____

_____

_____

_____

_____

_____

_____

Write Like a Reporter
Narrative Paragraph

Student Prompt, p. 106 Reread pp. 68–69 of *Hottest, Coldest, Highest, Deepest*. Write a tall tale using one of the places described in the text as your setting. Use evidence from the text and the illustrations to support the description of the setting in your story.

Writing to Sources Remind students that a tall tale is a humorous story that uses realistic details to tell about impossible characters and events. Have students look carefully at the text and illustrations in *Hottest, Coldest, Highest, Deepest* for details about the setting they chose. Point out that using these details as they write their tall tale will help them describe the realistic setting.

Students' tall tales should:

- use a place from the selection as the setting of the tale
- include realistic details to describe the setting
- introduce characters and events that are not realistic
- demonstrate strong command of the conventions of standard written English

Ⓒ **Common Core State Standards**

Writing 3. Write narratives to develop real or imagined experiences or events using effective technique, descriptive details, and clear event sequences.

Connect the Texts
Narrative Short Story

Student Prompt Look back at *Hottest, Coldest, Highest, Deepest* and "Paul Bunyan and the Great Lakes." Choose one setting from *Hottest, Coldest, Highest, Deepest* and write a short story in which Paul Bunyan creates the amazing feature of that setting. Use evidence from the texts to support your descriptions of the setting and the main character, Paul Bunyan.

_____

_____

_____

_____

_____

_____

_____

_____

_____

_____

_____

_____

_____

_____

_____

_____

Connect the Texts
Narrative Short Story

Student Prompt, p. 108 Look back at *Hottest, Coldest, Highest, Deepest* and "Paul Bunyan and the Great Lakes." Choose one setting from *Hottest, Coldest, Highest, Deepest* and write a short story in which Paul Bunyan creates the amazing feature of that setting. Use evidence from the texts to support your descriptions of the setting and the main character, Paul Bunyan.

Writing to Sources Ask students to fill in a story map before writing their short story. Have them use details from *Hottest, Coldest, Highest, Deepest* to support their description of the setting and details from "Paul Bunyan and the Great Lakes" to support their description of Paul Bunyan. Then have students brainstorm possible events for their story.

			4-point Narrative Writing Rubric		
Score	**Narrative Focus**	**Organization**	**Development of Narrative**	**Language and Vocabulary**	**Conventions**
4	Narrative is clearly focused and developed throughout.	Narrative has a well-developed, logical, easy-to-follow plot.	Narrative includes thorough and effective use of details, dialogue, and description.	Narrative uses precise, concrete sensory language as well as figurative language and/or domain-specific vocabulary.	Narrative has correct grammar, usage, spelling, capitalization, and punctuation.
3	Narrative is mostly focused and developed throughout.	Narrative has a plot, but there may be some lack of clarity and/or unrelated events.	Narrative includes adequate use of details, dialogue and description.	Narrative uses adequate sensory and figurative language and/or domain-specific vocabulary.	Narrative has a few errors but is completely understandable.
2	Narrative is somewhat developed but may occasionally lose focus.	Narrative's plot is difficult to follow, and ideas are not connected well.	Narrative includes only a few details, dialogues, and descriptions.	Language in narrative is not precise or sensory; lacks domain-specific vocabulary.	Narrative has some errors in usage, grammar, spelling and/or punctuation.
1	Narrative may be confusing, unfocused, or too short.	Narrative has little or no apparent plot.	Narrative includes few or no details, dialogue or description.	Language in narrative is vague, unclear, or confusing.	Narrative is hard to follow because of frequent errors.
0	Narrative gets no credit if it does not demonstrate adequate command of narrative writing traits.				

© Common Core State Standards

Writing 3. Write narratives to develop real or imagined experiences or events using effective technique, descriptive details, and clear event sequences.

Write Like a Reporter
Narrative Paragraph

Student Prompt Reread pp. 102–104 of *Rocks in His Head*. Make inferences about the narrator's father and Mrs. Johnson based on evidence in the text. Use these inferences to retell the ending of the story from Mrs. Johnson's point of view. Make sure the events in your story follow the events in the text.

_____

_____

_____

_____

_____

_____

_____

_____

_____

_____

_____

_____

_____

_____

_____

_____

_____

_____

Name _____

Write Like a Reporter
Narrative Paragraph

> **Student Prompt, p. 110** Reread pp. 102–104 of *Rocks in His Head*. Make inferences about the narrator's father and Mrs. Johnson based on evidence in the text. Use these inferences to retell the ending of the story from Mrs. Johnson's point of view. Make sure the events in your story follow the events in the text.

Writing to Sources Remind students that an inference is a conclusion we draw based on information we find in a text. Point out that to make and support valid inferences about the characters in *Rocks in His Head*, students will need to reread the text, looking closely at what the author has the characters say and do. Explain that students can use the inferences they make to support their characterizations as they retell the ending of the story from Mrs. Johnson's point of view.

Students' stories should:
- retell the ending of the selection from Mrs. Johnson's point of view
- follow a clear and structured sequence of events
- develop characters using dialogue and descriptions
- demonstrate strong command of the conventions of standard written English

© Common Core State Standards

Writing 3. Write narratives to develop real or imagined experiences or events using effective technique, descriptive details, and clear event sequences.

Connect the Texts
Narrative Story

Student Prompt Look back at *Rocks in His Head* and "Marvelous Marble Mania." Imagine the narrator's father in *Rocks in His Head* collects marbles instead of rocks. Use evidence from both texts, including inferences you made about the narrator's father, to write a story in which he collects marbles from around the world.

_____

_____

_____

_____

_____

_____

_____

_____

_____

_____

_____

_____

_____

_____

_____

_____

Connect the Texts

Narrative Story

Student Prompt, p. 112 Look back at *Rocks in His Head* and "Marvelous Marble Mania." Imagine the narrator's father in *Rocks in His Head* collects marbles instead of rocks. Use evidence from both texts, including inferences you made about the narrator's father, to write a story in which he collects marbles from around the world.

Writing to Sources Have students discuss how rocks and marbles are alike and how they are different, citing evidence from both texts. Then have students discuss their inferences about the narrator's father in *Rocks in His Head*. Tell students to use their inferences about the character and what they learned about marbles as they write their story.

	4-point Narrative Writing Rubric				
Score	**Narrative Focus**	**Organization**	**Development of Narrative**	**Language and Vocabulary**	**Conventions**
4	Narrative is clearly focused and developed throughout.	Narrative has a well-developed, logical, easy-to-follow plot.	Narrative includes thorough and effective use of details, dialogue, and description.	Narrative uses precise, concrete sensory language as well as figurative language and/or domain-specific vocabulary.	Narrative has correct grammar, usage, spelling, capitalization, and punctuation.
3	Narrative is mostly focused and developed throughout.	Narrative has a plot, but there may be some lack of clarity and/or unrelated events.	Narrative includes adequate use of details, dialogue and description.	Narrative uses adequate sensory and figurative language and/or domain-specific vocabulary.	Narrative has a few errors but is completely understandable.
2	Narrative is somewhat developed but may occasionally lose focus.	Narrative's plot is difficult to follow, and ideas are not connected well.	Narrative includes only a few details, dialogues, and descriptions.	Language in narrative is not precise or sensory; lacks domain-specific vocabulary.	Narrative has some errors in usage, grammar, spelling and/or punctuation.
1	Narrative may be confusing, unfocused, or too short.	Narrative has little or no apparent plot.	Narrative includes few or no details, dialogue or description.	Language in narrative is vague, unclear, or confusing.	Narrative is hard to follow because of frequent errors.
0	Narrative gets no credit if it does not demonstrate adequate command of narrative writing traits.				

© **Common Core State Standards**

Writing 3. Write narratives to develop real or imagined experiences or events using effective technique, descriptive details, and clear event sequences.

Write Like a Reporter
Narrative Paragraph

Student Prompt Reread p. 127 of *America's Champion Swimmer: Gertrude Ederle*. Write a realistic story about Trudy's first swimming lesson. Use evidence from the text to help you describe the characters, setting, and events.

_____

_____

_____

_____

_____

_____

_____

_____

_____

_____

_____

_____

_____

_____

_____

_____

_____

_____

Write Like a Reporter
Narrative Paragraph

Student Prompt, p. 114 Reread p. 127 of *America's Champion Swimmer: Gertrude Ederle*. Write a realistic story about Trudy's first swimming lesson. Use evidence from the text to help you describe the characters, setting, and events.

Writing to Sources Have students look carefully at the description of Trudy's first swimming lesson for details about the characters, setting, and events. Point out that students can use these details to help them as they write their story.

Students' stories should:

- tell about the swimming lesson described in the selection
- follow a clear and structured sequence of events
- use descriptive details to develop the setting and characters
- demonstrate strong command of the conventions of standard written English

© **Common Core State Standards**

Writing 3. Write narratives to develop real or imagined experiences or events using effective technique, descriptive details, and clear event sequences.

Connect the Texts
Narrative Short Story

Student Prompt Look back at *America's Champion Swimmer: Gertrude Ederle* and "Women Athletes." Write a short story in which Gertrude Ederle and Wilma Rudolph are the main characters. Use evidence from both texts to support the characterizations in your story.

_____

_____

_____

_____

_____

_____

_____

_____

_____

_____

_____

_____

_____

_____

_____

_____

_____

_____

Connect the Texts
Narrative Short Story

> **Student Prompt, p. 116** Look back at *America's Champion Swimmer: Gertrude Ederle* and "Women Athletes." Write a short story in which Gertrude Ederle and Wilma Rudolph are the main characters. Use evidence from both texts to support the characterizations in your story.

Writing to Sources Discuss with students what they know about Gertrude Ederle and Wilma Rudolph. Ask them to cite text evidence to support their characterizations. Point out that students can use this evidence to help them describe their characters as they write a story about Gertrude and Wilma. If necessary, brainstorm possible events and list them on the board.

	4-point Narrative Writing Rubric				
Score	Narrative Focus	Organization	Development of Narrative	Language and Vocabulary	Conventions
4	Narrative is clearly focused and developed throughout.	Narrative has a well-developed, logical, easy-to-follow plot.	Narrative includes thorough and effective use of details, dialogue, and description.	Narrative uses precise, concrete sensory language as well as figurative language and/or domain-specific vocabulary.	Narrative has correct grammar, usage, spelling, capitalization, and punctuation.
3	Narrative is mostly focused and developed throughout.	Narrative has a plot, but there may be some lack of clarity and/or unrelated events.	Narrative includes adequate use of details, dialogue and description.	Narrative uses adequate sensory and figurative language and/or domain-specific vocabulary.	Narrative has a few errors but is completely understandable.
2	Narrative is somewhat developed but may occasionally lose focus.	Narrative's plot is difficult to follow, and ideas are not connected well.	Narrative includes only a few details, dialogues, and descriptions.	Language in narrative is not precise or sensory; lacks domain-specific vocabulary.	Narrative has some errors in usage, grammar, spelling and/or punctuation.
1	Narrative may be confusing, unfocused, or too short.	Narrative has little or no apparent plot.	Narrative includes few or no details, dialogue or description.	Language in narrative is vague, unclear, or confusing.	Narrative is hard to follow because of frequent errors.
0	Narrative gets no credit if it does not demonstrate adequate command of narrative writing traits.				

© **Common Core State Standards**

Writing 3. Write narratives to develop real or imagined experiences or events using effective technique, descriptive details, and clear event sequences.

Write Like a Reporter
Narrative Paragraph

Student Prompt Reread pp. 164–171 of *Fly, Eagle, Fly!* Make inferences about the farmer's friend based on evidence in the text. Then imagine that the eagle does not fly away from the cliff. Write a story telling what the farmer's friend will do next to prove the bird is an eagle. Make sure the events in your story follow logically from the events in the tale.

_____

_____

_____

_____

_____

_____

_____

_____

_____

_____

_____

_____

_____

_____

_____

_____

_____

Write Like a Reporter
Narrative Paragraph

Student Prompt, p. 118 Reread pp. 164–171 of *Fly, Eagle, Fly!* Make inferences about the farmer's friend based on evidence in the text. Then imagine that the eagle does not fly away from the cliff. Write a story telling what the farmer's friend will do next to prove the bird is an eagle. Make sure the events in your story follow logically from the events in the tale.

Writing to Sources Remind students that to make and support valid inferences about the characters in *Fly, Eagle, Fly!* they will need to reread the text carefully, looking at what the author has the characters say and do. Tell students they can use their inferences about the farmer's friend to help them as they write a story telling what he will do next.

Students' stories should:

- tell what the farmer's friend will do next to prove the bird is an eagle
- provide descriptive details and dialogue that provide an accurate characterization of the farmer's friend
- include an event sequence that unfolds logically from the selection
- demonstrate strong command of the conventions of standard written English

---

© Common Core State Standards

Writing 3. Write narratives to develop real or imagined experiences or events using effective technique, descriptive details, and clear event sequences.

Connect the Texts
Narrative Story

Student Prompt Look back at *Fly, Eagle, Fly!* and "Purple Coyote." Imagine the farmer's friend meets the coyote. Do you think he will fall for the coyote's trick? Use details from both texts to make inferences about the characters. Then write a story telling what happens when they meet.

_____

_____

_____

_____

_____

_____

_____

_____

_____

_____

_____

_____

_____

_____

_____

_____

Connect the Texts
Narrative Story

Student Prompt, p. 120 Look back at *Fly, Eagle, Fly!* and "Purple Coyote." Imagine the farmer's friend meets the coyote. Do you think he will fall for the coyote's trick? Use details from both texts to make inferences about the characters. Then write a story telling what happens when they meet.

Writing to Sources Remind students that they can use details from the texts to make inferences about the two characters. Have them organize any details they find and inferences they make about the characters in a T-chart. Then have students write a story in which the two characters meet. Suggest that they use dialogue from both texts as a model for any dialogue they decide to write.

4-point Narrative Writing Rubric					
Score	**Narrative Focus**	**Organization**	**Development of Narrative**	**Language and Vocabulary**	**Conventions**
4	Narrative is clearly focused and developed throughout.	Narrative has a well-developed, logical, easy-to-follow plot.	Narrative includes thorough and effective use of details, dialogue, and description.	Narrative uses precise, concrete sensory language as well as figurative language and/or domain-specific vocabulary.	Narrative has correct grammar, usage, spelling, capitalization, and punctuation.
3	Narrative is mostly focused and developed throughout.	Narrative has a plot, but there may be some lack of clarity and/or unrelated events.	Narrative includes adequate use of details, dialogue and description.	Narrative uses adequate sensory and figurative language and/or domain-specific vocabulary.	Narrative has a few errors but is completely understandable.
2	Narrative is somewhat developed but may occasionally lose focus.	Narrative's plot is difficult to follow, and ideas are not connected well.	Narrative includes only a few details, dialogues, and descriptions.	Language in narrative is not precise or sensory; lacks domain-specific vocabulary.	Narrative has some errors in usage, grammar, spelling and/or punctuation.
1	Narrative may be confusing, unfocused, or too short.	Narrative has little or no apparent plot.	Narrative includes few or no details, dialogue or description.	Language in narrative is vague, unclear, or confusing.	Narrative is hard to follow because of frequent errors.
0	Narrative gets no credit if it does not demonstrate adequate command of narrative writing traits.				

© **Common Core State Standards**

Writing 3. Write narratives to develop real or imagined experiences or events using effective technique, descriptive details, and clear event sequences.

Prove It!
Realistic Narrative

Academic Vocabulary

In a **realistic narrative**, a writer tells a fictional story about characters that could exist and events that could happen. The events show how the main character solves a problem. The events may be told in straight chronological order or in another time order in which the chronology is made clear.

ELL

Introduce Genre Write *realistic narrative* on the board. Explain that this phrase is used to describe a fictional story that features characters, settings, and events that seem real. Point out that the events of a realistic narrative show how the main character solves a problem. Discuss with students the key features of a realistic narrative that appear on this page.

Success!

Realistic Narrative

In this unit, students have read examples of narrative writing, including a legend, a folk tale, and a trickster tale, and have had the opportunity to write in this mode. Remind students of texts and writing tasks (such as Write Like a Reporter and Connect the Texts) in which they have encountered and practiced narrative writing.

Key Features of a Realistic Narrative

- features made-up characters who are similar to real people and a setting that exists or could exist
- describes a problem faced by the characters
- focuses on a series of events that describes how the characters' problem is solved
- develops the story with dialogue, description, and narration
- uses words such as *first, later,* and *then* to indicate chronological order
- uses precise language and domain-specific vocabulary
- provides a conclusion that is reasonable and believable

Writing Task Overview

Each unit writing task provides students with an opportunity to write to sources. To successfully complete the task, students must analyze, synthesize, and evaluate multiple complex texts and create their own written response.

Success!

Part 1: Students will read and take notes on the selected sources. They will then respond to several questions about these sources and discuss their written responses with partners or in small groups.

Part 2: Students will work individually to plan, write, and revise their own realistic narrative.

Scorable Products: evidence-based short responses, realistic narrative

Success!: Writing Task – Short Response

Teacher Directions:

1. Introduce the Sources Refer students to the following texts in the Student Edition:

1. *The Man Who Invented Basketball,* pp. 28–41

2. *Rocks in His Head,* pp. 94–105

3. *America's Champion Swimmer: Gertrude Ederle,* pp. 124–139

Explain to students that they will need to draw evidence and support from the texts above in order to answer evidence-based short response questions and to write a realistic narrative. Students should take notes and categorize information as they closely reread the texts. Students should be given paper or a relevant graphic organizer from the TR DVD for note-taking.

2. Provide Student Directions and Scoring Information (p. 126) Answer any task-related questions students may have. If necessary, provide additional paper for students to write their responses.

3. Initiate the Writing Task If you are timing this part of the task, you may wish to alert students when half the allotted time has elapsed and again when 5 minutes remain.

4. Facilitate Collaboration After students have completed their written responses to the evidence-based short response questions, assign partners or small groups and have them discuss their responses. If students struggle to work together productively, provide them with tips and strategies for expressing their ideas and building on others'.

© **Common Core State Standards**

Writing 3. Write narratives to develop real or imagined experiences or events using effective technique, descriptive details, and clear event sequences. **Speaking/Listening 1.** Engage effectively in a range of collaborative discussions (one-on-one, in groups, and teacher-led) with diverse partners on grade 3 topics and texts, building on others' ideas and expressing their own clearly. **(Also Writing 3.a., Writing 3.b., Writing 3.d.)**

Scoring Information

Use the following 2-point scoring rubrics to evaluate students' answers to the evidence-based short response questions.

1. Compare the goals and the problems that the characters and people must overcome in the three selections. How are the their goals and difficulties similar and different?

Analysis Rubric	
2	The response: • demonstrates the ability to analyze similarities and differences among the characters in the texts • includes specific details that make reference to the texts
1	The response: • demonstrates a limited ability to analyze similarities and differences among the characters in the texts • includes some details that make reference to the texts
0	A response receives no credit if it demonstrates no ability to analyze similarities and differences among the characters in the texts or includes no relevant details from the texts.

2. Compile a list of personality traits that help people overcome difficulties. Cite examples from the texts of traits that helped the characters or people solve their problems.

Synthesis Rubric	
2	The response: • demonstrates the ability to synthesize information from the sources in order to compile a list of traits • includes specific details that make reference to the texts
1	The response: • demonstrates a limited ability to synthesize information from the sources in order to compile a list of traits • includes some details that make reference to the texts
0	A response receives no credit if it demonstrates no ability to synthesize information from the sources in order to compile a list of traits

3. Which character or person that you read about was the most successful? Defend your answer by citing evidence from the texts.

	Evaluation Rubric
2	The response: • demonstrates the ability to evaluate texts to determine levels of success • includes specific details that make reference to the texts
1	The response: • demonstrates a limited ability to evaluate texts to determine levels of success • includes some details that make reference to the texts
0	A response receives no credit if it demonstrates no ability to evaluate texts to determine levels of success.

Success!
Writing Task – Short Response

Student Directions:

Your assignment You will reread several selections from Unit 4 and take notes on these sources. Then you will answer three questions about these materials. You may refer to your notes or to any of the sources as often as you like.

Sources

1. *The Man Who Invented Basketball,* pp. 28–41

2. *Rocks in His Head,* pp. 94–105

3. *America's Champion Swimmer: Gertrude Ederle,* pp. 124–139

Be sure to read closely and take good notes. Your sources and notes will be the basis for writing your own realistic narrative in the second half of this writing task.

Evidence-Based Short Response Questions Answer the short response questions on the lines provided below each question. Your answers to these questions will be scored. Be sure to base your answers on the sources you have just read. Remember that you may refer back to your notes or to any of the sources.

After you have answered the questions, you will discuss your responses with a partner or in a small group. Your teacher will let you know when to begin the discussion part of this task.

Scoring Information Your responses will be scored based on how you demonstrate the ability to:

- compare and contrast across texts
- create a list based on information from all three texts
- choose the character or person you feel was most successful and tell why
- include specific details that clearly reference the sources

Evidence-Based Short Response Questions

1. Compare the goals and the problems that the characters and people must overcome in the three selections. How are their goals and difficulties similar and different?

_____

_____

_____

_____

2. Compile a list of personality traits that help people overcome difficulties. Cite examples from the texts of traits that helped the characters or people solve their problems.

_____

_____

_____

_____

3. Which character or person that you read about was the most successful? Defend your answer by citing evidence from the texts.

_____

_____

_____

_____

Collaborative Discussion

After you have written your responses to the questions, discuss your ideas. Your teacher will assign you a partner or a small group and let you know when to begin.

Success!: Writing Task – Realistic Narrative

Teacher Directions:

1. Provide Student Directions and Scoring Information (p. 130) Explain to students that they will now review their notes and sources and plan, draft, and revise their realistic narratives. Although they may use their notes and sources, they must work alone. Students will be allowed to look back at the answers they wrote to the short response questions, but they are not allowed to make changes to those answers. Have students read the directions for the realistic narrative and answer any task-related questions they may have. Students should be given paper on which to write their realistic narratives.

2. Initiate the Writing Task If you are timing this part of the task, you may wish to suggest approximate times for students to begin writing and revising. If students wish to continue writing rather than revising, allow them to do so. Alert students when 5 minutes remain.

3. Scoring Information Use the scoring rubric on the next page to evaluate students' realistic narratives.

4. Realistic Narrative Prompt Use what you have learned from reading *The Man Who Invented Basketball, Rocks in His Head,* and *America's Champion Swimmer: Gertrude Ederle* to write a realistic narrative about a person who overcomes difficulties and works hard to become successful. Be sure to follow the conventions of written English.

4-Point Narrative Writing Rubric				
Score	**Narrative Focus**	**Organization**	**Development of Narrative**	**Language and Vocabulary**	**Conventions**
4	Narrative is strongly focused and developed.	Narrative has a carefully developed and logical plot.	Narrative includes very effective use of details, dialogue, and description.	Narrative uses precise sensory language and/or domain-specific vocabulary.	Use of conventions is clearly shown.
3	Narrative is mostly focused and developed.	Narrative has a plot, but lacks clarity by using unrelated events.	Narrative includes adequate use of details, dialogue, and description.	Narrative uses adequate sensory language and/or domain-specific vocabulary.	Use of conventions is somewhat shown.
2	Narrative is somewhat developed but occasionally loses focus.	Narrative's plot is difficult to follow; ideas are not connected well.	Narrative includes only a few details, dialogues, and descriptions.	Language in narrative is not sensory; lacks domain-specific vocabulary.	Use of conventions is uneven.
1	Narrative may be confusing or unfocused.	Narrative has little or no apparent plot.	Narrative includes few or no details, dialogue, and description.	Language in narrative is vague, unclear.	There is very little correct use of conventions.
0	Narrative receives no credit if it does not demonstrate adequate command of narrative writing traits.				

ⓒ Common Core State Standards

Writing 3. Write narratives to develop real or imagined experiences or events using effective technique, descriptive details, and clear event sequences. **(Also Writing 3.a., Writing 3.b., Writing 3.d.)**

Success!
Writing Task – Realistic Narrative

Student Directions:

Your assignment Now you will review your notes and sources and plan, draft, and revise your realistic narrative. While you may use your notes and refer to the sources, you must work on your own. You may also refer to the answers you wrote to earlier questions, but you cannot change those answers.

Realistic Narrative Prompt Use what you have learned from reading *The Man Who Invented Basketball, Rocks in His Head,* and *America's Champion Swimmer: Gertrude Ederle* to write a realistic narrative about a person who overcomes difficulties and works hard to become successful. Be sure to follow the conventions of written English.

Scoring Information

Your realistic narrative will be assigned a score for

1. **Focus** – how well you maintain your focus and convey story events clearly

2. **Organization** – how well the events are described in time order

3. **Development** – how well you develop the story with dialogue, descriptions of characters and their actions, and details about the setting

4. **Language and Vocabulary** – how well you relate the story using precise language and domain-specific vocabulary

5. **Conventions** – how well you follow the rules of usage, punctuation, capitalization, and spelling

Now begin work on your realistic narrative. Try to manage your time carefully so that you can

- plan your realistic narrative

- write your realistic narrative

- revise and edit for a final draft

Success!: Writing Task – Realistic Narrative

Teacher Directions:

1. Publish Explain to students that publishing their writing is the last step in the writing process. If time permits, have students review one another's compositions and incorporate any comments their classmates have. Discuss different ways technology can be used to publish writing.

2. Present Students will now have the option to present their realistic narratives. Have students tell their stories in front of the class. Use the list below to offer students tips on listening and speaking.

While Listening to a Classmate...

- Face the speaker to listen attentively.
- Take notes on what the speaker says.

While Speaking to Classmates...

- Determine your purpose for speaking.
- Have good posture and eye contact.
- Speak at an appropriate pace.

Things to Do Together...

- Ask and answer questions with detail.
- Build on each other's ideas.

© Common Core State Standards

Writing 6. With guidance and support from adults, use technology to produce and publish writing (using keyboarding skills) as well as to interact and collaborate with others. **Speaking/Listening 4.** Report on a topic or text, tell a story, or recount an experience with appropriate facts and relevant, descriptive details, speaking clearly at an understandable pace.

Unit 5 Cultures

Writing Focus: Argument

Write Like a Reporter
Argumentative Paragraph

Student Prompt Reread the story *Suki's Kimono*. Who do you think enjoyed the first day of school more—Suki or her sisters? Write an opinion piece in which you state and defend your opinion. Provide evidence from the text to support your opinion.

_____

_____

_____

_____

_____

_____

_____

_____

_____

_____

_____

_____

_____

_____

_____

_____

_____

_____

_____

_____

Write Like a Reporter
Argumentative Paragraph

Student Prompt, p. 134 Reread the story *Suki's Kimono*. Who do you think enjoyed the first day of school more—Suki or her sisters? Write an opinion piece in which you state and defend your opinion. Provide evidence from the text to support your opinion.

Writing to Sources Have students reread the text carefully, looking at words and phrases that tell how Suki and her sisters feel about their first day at school. Point out that students can use these words and phrases to support their opinion.

Students' opinion pieces should:
- clearly state who enjoyed the first day of school more
- use words and phrases from the selection to support their opinion
- link opinion and reasons with words and phrases such as *because* and *since*
- demonstrate strong command of the conventions of standard written English

---

Ⓒ **Common Core State Standards**

Writing 1. Write opinion pieces on topics or texts, supporting a point of view with reasons.

Connect the Texts
Argumentative Essay

Student Prompt Look back at *Suki's Kimono* and "Clothes: Bringing Cultures Together." Which article of clothing would you most like to wear—the kimono from the first selection or the poncho, moccasins, or beret from the second selection? Provide evidence from both texts to support your opinion.

_____

_____

_____

_____

_____

_____

_____

_____

_____

_____

_____

_____

_____

_____

_____

_____

_____

_____

Connect the Texts
Argumentative Essay

Student Prompt, p. 136 Look back at *Suki's Kimono* and "Clothes: Bringing Cultures Together." Which article of clothing would you most like to wear—the kimono from the first selection or the poncho, moccasins, or beret from the second selection? Provide evidence from both texts to support your opinion.

Writing to Sources Discuss with students what they learned from the texts about the different kinds of clothing. Have them go back into both texts and find specific evidence to support their choice of clothing. Remind students to state their opinion clearly and to support it with two or three reasons that include details from both texts.

Score	Statement of Purpose/Focus	Organization	Development of Evidence	Language and Vocabulary	Conventions
4-point Argument Writing Rubric					
4	Opinion is clearly conveyed and well supported; response is focused.	Organization is clear and effective, creating a sense of cohesion.	Evidence is thorough and persuasive, and includes facts and details.	Ideas are clearly and effectively conveyed, using precise language and/or domain-specific vocabulary.	Command of conventions is strongly demonstrated.
3	Opinion is clear, adequately supported; response is generally focused.	Organization is clear, though minor flaws may be present and some ideas may be disconnected.	Evidence is adequate and includes facts and details.	Ideas are adequately conveyed, using both precise and more general language; may include domain-specific vocabulary.	Command of conventions is sufficiently demonstrated.
2	Opinion is somewhat supported; response may lack focus or include unnecessary material.	Organization is inconsistent, and flaws are apparent.	Evidence is uneven or incomplete; insufficient use of facts and details.	Ideas are unevenly conveyed, using overly-simplistic language; lack of domain-specific vocabulary.	Command of conventions is uneven.
1	The response may be confusing, unfocused; opinion not sufficiently supported.	Organization is poor or nonexistent.	Evidence is poor or nonexistent.	Ideas are conveyed in a vague, unclear, or confusing manner.	There is very little command of conventions.
0	The response shows no evidence of the ability to construct a coherent opinion essay using information from sources.				

© **Common Core State Standards**

Writing 1. Write opinion pieces on topics or texts, supporting a point of view with reasons.

Write Like a Reporter
Argumentative Paragraph

Student Prompt Reread the story *I Love Saturdays y domingos*. Which part of her Saturdays and domingos do you think the girl likes best? Draw a conclusion based on details in the text. Write an opinion piece in which you state and defend your conclusion. Support your opinion with text evidence.

_____

_____

_____

_____

_____

_____

_____

_____

_____

_____

_____

_____

_____

_____

_____

_____

_____

Write Like a Reporter
Argumentative Paragraph

Student Prompt, p. 138 Reread the story *I Love Saturdays y domingos.* Which part of her Saturdays and domingos do you think the girl likes best? Draw a conclusion based on details in the text. Write an opinion piece in which you state and defend your conclusion. Support your opinion with text evidence.

Writing to Sources Have students reread the text carefully, paying attention to what the girl says and does. Point out that students can use these details to draw a conclusion about what she likes best. Remind students to state their opinion clearly and then provide two or three reasons that are supported by evidence from the text.

Students' opinion pieces should:

- clearly state which part of her Saturdays and domingos the girl likes best
- base their opinion on conclusions drawn from the selection
- provide reasons supported by evidence from the text
- demonstrate strong command of the conventions of standard written English

© **Common Core State Standards**

Writing 1. Write opinion pieces on topics or texts, supporting a point of view with reasons.

Connect the Texts
Argumentative Essay

Student Prompt Look back at the girl's birthday celebration in *I Love Saturdays y domingos* and the celebrations in "Communities Celebrate Cultures." Which celebration do you think sounds most interesting? Why? Write your opinion and provide supporting evidence from both texts.

_____

_____

_____

_____

_____

_____

_____

_____

_____

_____

_____

_____

_____

_____

_____

_____

_____

Connect the Texts
Argumentative Essay

Student Prompt, p. 140 Look back at the girl's birthday celebration in *I Love Saturdays y domingos* and the celebrations in "Communities Celebrate Cultures." Which celebration do you think sounds most interesting? Why? Write your opinion and provide supporting evidence from both texts.

Writing to Sources Review both selections with students, focusing on the description of each celebration. Suggest that students create a list of things they like or dislike about each celebration. Then have them write their opinion and use the lists to choose evidence to support their opinion.

	4-point Argument Writing Rubric				
Score	**Statement of Purpose/Focus**	**Organization**	**Development of Evidence**	**Language and Vocabulary**	**Conventions**
4	Opinion is clearly conveyed and well supported; response is focused.	Organization is clear and effective, creating a sense of cohesion.	Evidence is thorough and persuasive, and includes facts and details.	Ideas are clearly and effectively conveyed, using precise language and/or domain-specific vocabulary.	Command of conventions is strongly demonstrated.
3	Opinion is clear, adequately supported; response is generally focused.	Organization is clear, though minor flaws may be present and some ideas may be disconnected.	Evidence is adequate and includes facts and details.	Ideas are adequately conveyed, using both precise and more general language; may include domain-specific vocabulary.	Command of conventions is sufficiently demonstrated.
2	Opinion is somewhat supported; response may lack focus or include unnecessary material.	Organization is inconsistent, and flaws are apparent.	Evidence is uneven or incomplete; insufficient use of facts and details.	Ideas are unevenly conveyed, using overly-simplistic language; lack of domain-specific vocabulary.	Command of conventions is uneven.
1	The response may be confusing, unfocused; opinion not sufficiently supported.	Organization is poor or nonexistent.	Evidence is poor or nonexistent.	Ideas are conveyed in a vague, unclear, or confusing manner.	There is very little command of conventions.
0	The response shows no evidence of the ability to construct a coherent opinion essay using information from sources.				

© **Common Core State Standards**

Writing 1. Write opinion pieces on topics or texts, supporting a point of view with reasons.

Write Like a Reporter
Argumentative Paragraph

Student Prompt Reread the story *Good-Bye, 382 Shin Dang Dong.* Do you think it will be easy or difficult for Jangmi to adapt to a new culture? Write your opinion. Find and write at least three good reasons from the text to support your opinion.

_____

_____

_____

_____

_____

_____

_____

_____

_____

_____

_____

_____

_____

_____

_____

Write Like a Reporter
Argumentative Paragraph

> **Student Prompt, p. 142** Reread the story *Good-Bye, 382 Shin Dang Dong.* Do you think it will be easy or difficult for Jangmi to adapt to a new culture? Write your opinion. Find and write at least three good reasons from the text to support your opinion.

Writing to Sources Point out to students that they will need to reread the text carefully, looking for words and sentences they can use as evidence to support their opinion. Tell them to first state their opinion clearly and then to provide two or three reasons supported by details from the text. If students have difficulty finding evidence in the text, guide them to reread pp. 275–278.

Students' opinion pieces should:

- clearly state whether it will be easy or difficult for Jangmi to adapt to a new culture
- use words and sentences from the selection to support their opinion
- link opinion and reasons with words and phrases such as *for example* and *therefore*
- demonstrate strong command of the conventions of standard written English

---

Ⓒ **Common Core State Standards**

Writing 1. Write opinion pieces on topics or texts, supporting a point of view with reasons.

Connect the Texts
Argumentative Opinion Piece

Student Prompt Look back at *Good-Bye, 382 Shin Dang Dong* and "Sing a Song of People." Do you think Jangmi would enjoy living in the place described in the poem? Use details from both texts to draw a conclusion. Write an opinion piece in which you state and defend your conclusion using text evidence.

_____

_____

_____

_____

_____

_____

_____

_____

_____

_____

_____

_____

_____

_____

_____

_____

_____

Connect the Texts
Argumentative Opinion Piece

> **Student Prompt, p. 144** Look back at *Good-Bye, 382 Shin Dang Dong* and "Sing a Song of People." Do you think Jangmi would enjoy living in the place described in the poem? Use details from both texts to draw a conclusion. Write an opinion piece in which you state and defend your conclusion using text evidence.

Writing to Sources Discuss students' conclusions and the details they used to draw those conclusions. Have them go back into both texts and find specific evidence to support their opinion. Remind students to look closely at the authors' words and phrases and to think about the inferences readers can make from this language.

		4-point Argument Writing Rubric			
Score	**Statement of Purpose/Focus**	**Organization**	**Development of Evidence**	**Language and Vocabulary**	**Conventions**
4	Opinion is clearly conveyed and well supported; response is focused.	Organization is clear and effective, creating a sense of cohesion.	Evidence is thorough and persuasive, and includes facts and details.	Ideas are clearly and effectively conveyed, using precise language and/or domain-specific vocabulary.	Command of conventions is strongly demonstrated.
3	Opinion is clear, adequately supported; response is generally focused.	Organization is clear, though minor flaws may be present and some ideas may be disconnected.	Evidence is adequate and includes facts and details.	Ideas are adequately conveyed, using both precise and more general language; may include domain-specific vocabulary.	Command of conventions is sufficiently demonstrated.
2	Opinion is somewhat supported; response may lack focus or include unnecessary material.	Organization is inconsistent, and flaws are apparent.	Evidence is uneven or incomplete; insufficient use of facts and details.	Ideas are unevenly conveyed, using overly-simplistic language; lack of domain-specific vocabulary.	Command of conventions is uneven.
1	The response may be confusing, unfocused; opinion not sufficiently supported.	Organization is poor or nonexistent.	Evidence is poor or nonexistent.	Ideas are conveyed in a vague, unclear, or confusing manner.	There is very little command of conventions.
0	The response shows no evidence of the ability to construct a coherent opinion essay using information from sources.				

ⓒ Common Core State Standards

Writing 1. Write opinion pieces on topics or texts, supporting a point of view with reasons.

Write Like a Reporter
Argumentative Paragraph

Student Prompt Reread the selection *Jalapeño Bagels*. Do you think Pablo is proud that he comes from two different cultures? Write an opinion piece in which you state and defend your opinion using evidence from the text.

_____

_____

_____

_____

_____

_____

_____

_____

_____

_____

_____

_____

_____

_____

_____

_____

_____

_____

_____

Write Like a Reporter

Argumentative Paragraph

> **Student Prompt, p. 146** Reread the selection *Jalapeño Bagels.* Do you think Pablo is proud that he comes from two different cultures? Write an opinion piece in which you state and defend your opinion using evidence from the text.

Writing to Sources Point out to students that they can use details from the text to make inferences about Pablo's thoughts and feelings. Once they have stated their opinion clearly, students can use the evidence they find as well as their inferences to support their opinion with two or three reasons.

Students' paragraphs should:

- clearly state whether Pablo is proud that he comes from two different cultures
- use inferences about Pablo's thoughts and feelings to support their opinion
- provide reasons supported by details from the text
- demonstrate strong command of the conventions of standard written English

---

ⓒ Common Core State Standards

Writing 1. Write opinion pieces on topics or texts, supporting a point of view with reasons.

Connect the Texts
Argumentative Essay

Student Prompt Look back at *Jalapeño Bagels* and "Foods of Mexico."
Both selections tell about food that blends two cultures. Which food would
you rather try—the jalapeño bagel in the first selection or the torta de tamal
in the second selection? Write your opinion. Then provide details from both
texts as evidence to support your opinion.

_____

_____

_____

_____

_____

_____

_____

_____

_____

_____

_____

_____

_____

_____

_____

_____

Connect the Texts
Argumentative Essay

Student Prompt, p. 148 Look back at *Jalapeño Bagels* and "Foods of Mexico." Both selections tell about food that blends two cultures. Which food would you rather try—the jalapeño bagel in the first selection or the torta de tamal in the second selection? Write your opinion. Then provide details from both texts as evidence to support your opinion.

Writing to Sources Have students read both texts carefully for details about the jalapeño bagel and the torta de tamal. Suggest that students list their ideas as a way to help them form their opinion. Then have students write their opinion and choose evidence from the lists to support their opinion.

	4-point Argument Writing Rubric				
Score	**Statement of Purpose/Focus**	**Organization**	**Development of Evidence**	**Language and Vocabulary**	**Conventions**
4	Opinion is clearly conveyed and well supported; response is focused.	Organization is clear and effective, creating a sense of cohesion.	Evidence is thorough and persuasive, and includes facts and details.	Ideas are clearly and effectively conveyed, using precise language and/or domain-specific vocabulary.	Command of conventions is strongly demonstrated.
3	Opinion is clear, adequately supported; response is generally focused.	Organization is clear, though minor flaws may be present and some ideas may be disconnected.	Evidence is adequate and includes facts and details.	Ideas are adequately conveyed, using both precise and more general language; may include domain-specific vocabulary.	Command of conventions is sufficiently demonstrated.
2	Opinion is somewhat supported; response may lack focus or include unnecessary material.	Organization is inconsistent, and flaws are apparent.	Evidence is uneven or incomplete; insufficient use of facts and details.	Ideas are unevenly conveyed, using overly-simplistic language; lack of domain-specific vocabulary.	Command of conventions is uneven.
1	The response may be confusing, unfocused; opinion not sufficiently supported.	Organization is poor or nonexistent.	Evidence is poor or nonexistent.	Ideas are conveyed in a vague, unclear, or confusing manner.	There is very little command of conventions.
0	The response shows no evidence of the ability to construct a coherent opinion essay using information from sources.				

© Common Core State Standards

Writing 1. Write opinion pieces on topics or texts, supporting a point of view with reasons.

Write Like a Reporter
Argumentative Paragraph

> **Student Prompt** Reread the selection *Me and Uncle Romie*. In the beginning Daddy tells James that Uncle Romie is a good man. What makes Uncle Romie a good man? Write your opinion. Then look through the text for evidence that supports your opinion. Find and write at least three good reasons.

_____

_____

_____

_____

_____

_____

_____

_____

_____

_____

_____

_____

_____

_____

_____

_____

_____

_____

Write Like a Reporter
Argumentative Paragraph

> **Student Prompt, p. 150** Reread the selection *Me and Uncle Romie.* In the beginning Daddy tells James that Uncle Romie is a good man. What makes Uncle Romie a good man? Write your opinion. Then look through the text for evidence that supports your opinion. Find and write at least three good reasons.

Writing to Sources Suggest that students begin their opinion piece by answering the question: What makes Uncle Romie a good man? Then have students reread the text carefully, looking for reasons that support their opinion. If they have difficulty finding evidence in the text, guide them to reread pp. 342–348.

Students' opinion pieces should:

- clearly state why they think Uncle Romie is a good man
- follow their opinion with reasons supported by facts and details from the selection
- link opinion and reasons with words and phrases such as *one thing* and *another*
- demonstrate strong command of the conventions of standard written English

---

© Common Core State Standards

Writing 1. Write opinion pieces on topics or texts, supporting a point of view with reasons.

Connect the Texts
Argumentative Essay

Student Prompt Look back at *Me and Uncle Romie* and "Country to City." Both selections describe North Carolina and New York. Which do you think is a better place to live? Use information from both texts not only to support the place you chose but also to explain why you did not choose the other place. Use persuasive words to convince readers to agree with your choice.

_____

_____

_____

_____

_____

_____

_____

_____

_____

_____

_____

_____

_____

_____

_____

_____

_____

Connect the Texts
Argumentative Essay

Student Prompt, p. 152 Look back at *Me and Uncle Romie* and "Country to City." Both selections describe North Carolina and New York. Which do you think is a better place to live? Use information from both texts not only to support the place you chose but also to explain why you did not choose the other place. Use persuasive words to convince readers to agree with your choice.

Writing to Sources Have students review both texts and make a T-chart listing reasons why they would or would not like to live in each place. Tell them to first state their opinion clearly and then provide reasons supported by facts and details from both texts. Remind students to use persuasive words that will appeal to readers.

4-point Argument Writing Rubric					
Score	**Statement of Purpose/Focus**	**Organization**	**Development of Evidence**	**Language and Vocabulary**	**Conventions**
4	Opinion is clearly conveyed and well supported; response is focused.	Organization is clear and effective, creating a sense of cohesion.	Evidence is thorough and persuasive, and includes facts and details.	Ideas are clearly and effectively conveyed, using precise language and/or domain-specific vocabulary.	Command of conventions is strongly demonstrated.
3	Opinion is clear, adequately supported; response is generally focused.	Organization is clear, though minor flaws may be present and some ideas may be disconnected.	Evidence is adequate and includes facts and details.	Ideas are adequately conveyed, using both precise and more general language; may include domain-specific vocabulary.	Command of conventions is sufficiently demonstrated.
2	Opinion is somewhat supported; response may lack focus or include unnecessary material.	Organization is inconsistent, and flaws are apparent.	Evidence is uneven or incomplete; insufficient use of facts and details.	Ideas are unevenly conveyed, using overly-simplistic language; lack of domain-specific vocabulary.	Command of conventions is uneven.
1	The response may be confusing, unfocused; opinion not sufficiently supported.	Organization is poor or nonexistent.	Evidence is poor or nonexistent.	Ideas are conveyed in a vague, unclear, or confusing manner.	There is very little command of conventions.
0	The response shows no evidence of the ability to construct a coherent opinion essay using information from sources.				

© **Common Core State Standards**

Writing 1. Write opinion pieces on topics or texts, supporting a point of view with reasons.

Prove It!
Argumentative Essay

In an **argumentative essay**, a writer tries to convince a reader to act or believe in a certain way. The writer supports opionions with reasons, facts, and examples. The writer uses persuasive words to make the reasons more convincing.

ELL

Introduce Genre Write *argumentative essay* on the board. Explain that this phrase is used to describe writing that expresses the writer's personal views. Point out that an opinion should be supported by reasons that include facts and examples. Discuss with students the key features of an argumentative essay that appear on this page.

Learning About Other Cultures

Argumentative Essay

In this unit, students have read examples of argumentative, or opinion, writing, such as a letter to the editor and a book review, and have had the opportunity to write in this mode. Remind students of texts and writing tasks (such as Write Like a Reporter and Connect the Texts) in which they have encountered and practiced argumentative writing.

Key Features of an Argumentative Essay

- establishes a clear position on an issue or question
- supports the position with details, reasons, facts, and examples as evidence
- tries to convince readers to think or act in a certain way
- uses persuasive words to make reasons more convincing
- often organizes ideas and facts in order of importance
- provides a concluding statement or section related to the topic

Writing Task Overview

Each unit writing task provides students with an opportunity to write to sources. To successfully complete the task, students must analyze, synthesize, and evaluate multiple complex texts and create their own written response.

Learning About Other Cultures

Part 1: Students will read and take notes on the selected sources. They will then respond to several questions about these sources and discuss their written responses with partners or in small groups.

Part 2: Students will work individually to plan, write, and revise their own argumentative essay.

Scorable Products: evidence-based short responses, argumentative essay

Learning About Other Cultures: Writing Task – Short Response

Teacher Directions:

1. Introduce the Sources Refer students to the following texts in the Student Edition:

1. *Suki's Kimono*, pp. 198–211

2. *I Love Saturdays y domingos*, pp. 230–245

3. *Jalapeño Bagels*, pp. 296–309

Explain to students that they will need to draw evidence and support from the texts above in order to answer evidence-based short response questions and to write an argumentative essay. Students should take notes and categorize information as they closely reread the texts. Students should be given paper or a relevant graphic organizer from the TR DVD for note-taking.

2. Provide Student Directions and Scoring Information (p. 158) Answer any task-related questions students may have. If necessary, provide additional paper for students to write their responses.

3. Initiate the Writing Task If you are timing this part of the task, you may wish to alert students when half the allotted time has elapsed and again when 5 minutes remain.

4. Facilitate Collaboration After students have completed their written responses to the evidence-based short response questions, assign partners or small groups and have them discuss their responses. If students struggle to work together productively, provide them with tips and strategies for expressing their ideas and building on others'.

© Common Core State Standards

Writing 1. Write opinion pieces on topics or texts, supporting a point of view with reasons. **Writing 8.** Recall information from experiences or gather information from print and digital sources; take brief notes on sources and sort evidence into provided categories. **Speaking/Listening 1.** Engage effectively in a range of collaborative discussions (one-on-one, in groups, and teacher-led) with diverse partners on grade 3 topics and texts, building on others' ideas and expressing their own clearly. **(Also Writing 1.a., Writing 1.b., Writing 1.c., Writing 1.d.)**

Scoring Information

Use the following 2-point scoring rubrics to evaluate students' answers to the evidence-based short response questions.

1. Compare the parts of culture that the characters explore in the three stories. How are the parts of culture they explore similar and different?

Analysis Rubric	
2	The response: • demonstrates the ability to analyze similarities and differences among cultures in the texts • includes specific details that make reference to the texts
1	The response: • demonstrates a limited ability to analyze similarities and differences among cultures in the texts • includes some details that make reference to the texts
0	A response receives no credit if it demonstrates no ability to analyze similarities and differences among cultures in the texts or includes no relevant details from the texts.

2. What lesson do all the main characters in the stories learn? Give examples from the texts to support your answer.

Synthesis Rubric	
2	The response: • demonstrates the ability to synthesize information from the sources in order to evaluate a common theme • includes specific details that make reference to the texts
1	The response: • demonstrates a limited ability to synthesize information from the sources in order to evaluate a common theme • includes some details that make reference to the texts
0	A response receives no credit if it demonstrates no ability to synthesize information from the sources in order to evaluate a theme or includes no relevant details from the texts.

3. Tell how characters in the texts explore their cultures. Recommend the best way to learn about a culture. Support your recommendation with examples from the texts.

	Evaluation Rubric
2	The response: • demonstrates the ability to evaluate texts in order to recommend the best way to learn about a culture • includes specific details that make reference to the texts
1	The response: • demonstrates a limited ability to evaluate texts in order to recommend the best way to learn about a culture • includes some details that make reference to the texts
0	A response receives no credit if it demonstrates no ability to evaluate texts or includes no relevant details from the texts

Ⓒ **Common Core State Standards**

Writing 8. Recall information from experiences or gather information from print and digital sources; take brief notes on sources and sort evidence into provided categories.

Learning About Other Cultures
Writing Task – Short Response

Student Directions:

Your assignment You will reread several selections from Unit 5 and take notes on these sources. Then you will answer three questions about these materials. You may refer to your notes or to any of the sources as often as you like.

Sources

1. *Suki's Kimono,* pp. 198–211

2. *I Love Saturdays y domingos,* pp. 230–245

3. *Jalapeño Bagels,* pp. 296–309

Be sure to read closely and take good notes. Your sources and notes will be the basis for writing your own argumentative essay in the second half of this writing task.

Evidence-Based Short Response Questions Answer the short response questions on the lines provided below each question. Your answers to these questions will be scored. Be sure to base your answers on the sources you have just read. Remember that you may refer back to your notes or to any of the sources.

After you have answered the questions, you will discuss your responses with a partner or in a small group. Your teacher will let you know when to begin the discussion part of this task.

Scoring Information Your responses will be scored based on how you demonstrate the ability to:

- compare and contrast information across texts
- describe a lesson learned in all three texts
- make a recommendation and support it
- include specific details that clearly reference the sources

Evidence-Based Short Response Questions

1. Compare the parts of culture that the characters explore in the three stories. How are the parts of culture they explore similar and different?

_____

_____

_____

_____

2. What lesson do all the main characters in the stories learn? Give examples from the texts to support your answer.

_____

_____

_____

_____

3. Tell how characters in the texts explore their cultures. Recommend the best way to learn about a culture. Support your recommendation with examples from the texts.

_____

_____

_____

_____

Collaborative Discussion

After you have written your responses to the questions, discuss your ideas. Your teacher will assign you a partner or a small group and let you know when to begin.

Learning About Other Cultures: Writing Task – Argumentative Essay

Teacher Directions:

1. **Provide Student Directions and Scoring Information (p. 162)** Explain to students that they will now review their notes and sources and plan, draft, and revise their argumentative essays. Although they may use their notes and sources, they must work alone. Students will be allowed to look back at the answers they wrote to the short response questions, but they are not allowed to make changes to those answers. Have students read the directions for the argumentative essay and answer any task-related questions they may have. Students should be given paper on which to write their essays.

2. **Initiate the Writing Task** If you are timing this part of the task, you may wish to suggest approximate times for students to begin writing and revising. If students wish to continue writing rather than revising, allow them to do so. Alert students when 5 minutes remain.

3. **Scoring Information** Use the scoring rubric on the next page to evaluate students' argumentative essays.

4. **Argumentative Essay Prompt** Use what you learned by reading *Suki's Kimono*, *I Love Saturdays y domingos*, and *Jalapeño Bagels* to write an argumentative essay about why it's important to learn about different cultures. Develop your argument using text evidence from all three texts. Be sure to follow the conventions of written English.

4-point Argument Writing Rubric

Score	Statement of Purpose/Focus	Organization	Development of Evidence	Language and Vocabulary	Conventions
4	Opinion of literature is clearly conveyed and well supported.	Organization includes clear opinions, reasons, and concluding statement.	Evidence includes sufficient facts and details from sources; is thorough and persuasive.	Ideas are clearly conveyed, using persuasive words and linking words.	Use of conventions is clearly shown.
3	Opinion of literature is clear, adequately supported.	Organization is clear, though minor flaws may be present and some ideas may be disconnected.	Evidence is adequate and includes facts and details.	Ideas are adequately conveyed, using some persuasive words and linking words.	Command of conventions is sufficiently demonstrated.
2	Opinion of literature is somewhat supported and includes unnecessary material.	Organization is inconsistent, and flaws are apparent.	Evidence is uneven or incomplete; insufficient use of facts and details.	Ideas are unevenly conveyed, using simplistic language; lacks domain-specific vocabulary.	Command of conventions is uneven.
1	Response may be confusing; not sufficiently supported.	Organization is poor or nonexistent.	Evidence is poor or nonexistent.	Ideas are conveyed in a vague or confusing manner.	There is very little command of conventions.
0	The response demonstrates no evidence of the ability to construct a coherent opinion essay using information from sources.				

ⓒ Common Core State Standards

Writing 1. Write opinion pieces on topics or texts, supporting a point of view with reasons. **Writing 10.** Write routinely over extended time frames (time for research, reflection, and revision) and shorter time frames (a single sitting or a day or two) for a range of discipline-specific tasks, purposes, and audiences. **(Also Writing 1.a., Writing 1.b., Writing 1.c., Writing 1.d.)**

Name _____

Learning About Other Cultures
Writing Task – Argumentative Essay

Student Directions:

Your assignment Now you will review your notes and sources and plan, draft, and revise your argumentative essay. While you may use your notes and refer to the sources, you must work on your own. You may also refer to the answers you wrote to earlier questions, but you cannot change those answers.

Argumentative Essay Prompt Use what you learned by reading *Suki's Kimono*, *I Love Saturdays y domingos*, and *Jalapeño Bagels* to write an argumentative essay about why it's important to learn about different cultures. Develop your argument using text evidence from all three texts. Be sure to follow the conventions of written English.

Scoring Information Your argumentative essay will be assigned a score for

1. **Focus** – how well you maintain your focus on your opinion and the reasons for it

2. **Organization** – how well the reasons are organized

3. **Development** – how well you develop the essay with reasons that include facts and examples

4. **Language and Vocabulary** – how well you develop the essay using precise language and domain-specific vocabulary

5. **Conventions** – how well you follow the rules of usage, punctuation, capitalization, and spelling

Now begin work on your argumentative essay. Try to manage your time carefully so that you can

- plan your argumentative essay

- write your argumentative essay

- revise and edit for a final draft

Learning About Other Cultures: Writing Task – Argumentative Essay

Teacher Directions:

1. Publish Explain to students that publishing their writing is the last step in the writing process. If time permits, have students review one another's compositions and incorporate any comments their classmates have. Discuss different ways technology can be used to publish writing.

2. Present Students will now have the option to present their argumentative essays. Have students give speeches on their argumentative essays in front of the class. Use the list below to offer students some tips on listening and speaking.

While Listening to a Classmate...

- Face the speaker to listen attentively.
- Take notes on what the speaker says.

While Speaking to Classmates...

- Determine your purpose for speaking.
- Have good posture and eye contact.
- Speak at an appropriate pace.

Things to Do Together...

- Ask and answer questions with detail.
- Build on each other's ideas.

Ⓒ Common Core State Standards

Writing 6. With guidance and support from adults, use technology to produce and publish writing (using keyboarding skills) as well as to interact and collaborate with others. **Speaking/Listening 4.** Report on a topic or text, tell a story, or recount an experience with appropriate facts and relevant, descriptive details, speaking clearly at an understandable pace.

Unit 6 Freedom

Writing Focus: Informative/Explanatory

Write Like a Reporter
Informative/Explanatory Paragraph

Student Prompt Reread pp. 376–382 of *The Story of the Statue of Liberty*. Think about how the Statue of Liberty was built. Based on evidence in the text, write an explanation of the process as a series of steps, including what was involved in each step. Add time-order words to clarify the sequence of the steps.

_____

_____

_____

_____

_____

_____

_____

_____

_____

_____

_____

_____

_____

_____

_____

_____

_____

_____

Write Like a Reporter

Informative/Explanatory Paragraph

Student Prompt, p. 166 Reread pp. 376–382 of *The Story of the Statue of Liberty*. Think about how the Statue of Liberty was built. Based on evidence in the text, write an explanation of the process as a series of steps, including what was involved in each step. Add time-order words to clarify the sequence of the steps.

Writing to Sources Have students reread the text carefully to find the steps in the process of building the Statue of Liberty. Tell them to take notes as they read. Explain that these notes will help them organize their ideas and include facts and details from the text as they write their explanation. Remind students to use time-order words such as *first, next,* and *then.*

Students' explanations should:

- tell the steps in the process of building the Statue of Liberty
- provide facts and details to develop the topic and support their ideas
- include time-order words and phrases to clarify the sequence
- demonstrate strong command of the conventions of standard written English

© Common Core State Standards

Writing 2. Write informative/explanatory texts to examine a topic and convey ideas and information clearly.

Connect the Texts

Informative/Explanatory Paragraph

Student Prompt Look back at *The Story of the Statue of Liberty* and "A Nation of Immigrants." Find and list details that answer this question: What does the Statue of Liberty symbolize for immigrants coming to the United States? Write a short explanation using facts and details from both texts.

_____

_____

_____

_____

_____

_____

_____

_____

_____

_____

_____

_____

_____

_____

_____

_____

Connect the Texts

Informative/Explanatory Paragraph

> **Student Prompt, p. 168** Look back at *The Story of the Statue of Liberty* and "A Nation of Immigrants." Find and list details that answer this question: What does the Statue of Liberty symbolize for immigrants coming to the United States? Write a short explanation using facts and details from both texts.

Writing to Sources Have students return to both texts and list facts and details about the topic. Tell them they can use this list as they write their explanation. Encourage students to begin their explanation with a topic sentence, include supporting facts and details, and end with a concluding statement.

Informative/Explanatory Writing Rubric					
Score	Focus	Organization	Development of Evidence	Language and Vocabulary	Conventions
4	Main idea is clearly conveyed and well supported; response is focused.	Organization is clear and effective, creating a sense of cohesion.	Evidence is relevant and thorough; includes facts and details.	Ideas are clearly and effectively conveyed, using precise language and/or domain-specific vocabulary.	Command of conventions is strongly demonstrated.
3	Main idea is clear, adequately supported; response is generally focused.	Organization is clear, though minor flaws may be present and some ideas may be disconnected.	Evidence is adequate and includes facts and details.	Ideas are adequately conveyed, using both precise and more general language; may include domain-specific vocabulary.	Command of conventions is sufficiently demonstrated.
2	Main idea is somewhat supported; lacks focus or includes unnecessary material.	Organization is inconsistent, and flaws are apparent.	Evidence is uneven or incomplete; insufficient use of facts and details.	Ideas are unevenly conveyed, using overly-simplistic language; lacks domain-specific vocabulary.	Command of conventions is uneven.
1	Response may be confusing, unfocused; main idea insufficiently supported.	Organization is poor or nonexistent.	Evidence is poor or nonexistent.	Ideas are conveyed in a vague, unclear, or confusing manner.	There is very little command of conventions.
0	The response shows no evidence of the ability to construct a coherent explanatory essay using information from sources.				

© Common Core State Standards

Writing 2. Write informative/explanatory texts to examine a topic and convey ideas and information clearly.

Write Like a Reporter
Informative/Explanatory Paragraph

Student Prompt Reread the story *Happy Birthday Mr. Kang.* Look for details in the text and illustrations about life as a Chinese immigrant in the United States. Use these details to write a short report about Chinese food and customs and how cultures can blend.

_____

_____

_____

_____

_____

_____

_____

_____

_____

_____

_____

_____

_____

_____

_____

_____

_____

_____

Write Like a Reporter

Informative/Explanatory Paragraph

Student Prompt, p. 170 Reread the story *Happy Birthday Mr. Kang*. Look for details in the text and illustrations about life as a Chinese immigrant in the United States. Use these details to write a short report about Chinese food and customs and how cultures can blend.

Writing to Sources Have students reread the selection carefully and take notes on details they find about the lives of Chinese immigrants in the story. Tell them to organize these notes by topic and then arrange the topics in a logical order. Remind students to begin their report by stating the topic and to end with a concluding statement.

Students' reports should:

- tell about life as a Chinese immigrant in the United States
- follow an organizational structure that groups related information
- provide details to develop the topic and support their ideas
- demonstrate strong command of the conventions of standard written English

Writing 2. Write informative/explanatory texts to examine a topic and convey ideas and information clearly.

Connect the Texts
Informative/Explanatory Comparison

Student Prompt Compare and contrast *Happy Birthday Mr. Kang* and "Once Upon a Constitution." Look at their organization and purpose as well as their graphics and words. Write an explanation of how the selections are alike and different. Provide evidence from both texts to support your ideas.

_____

_____

_____

_____

_____

_____

_____

_____

_____

_____

_____

_____

_____

_____

_____

_____

_____

_____

Connect the Texts
Informative/Explanatory Comparison

> **Student Prompt, p. 172** Compare and contrast *Happy Birthday Mr. Kang* and "Once Upon a Constitution." Look at their organization and purpose as well as their graphics and words. Write an explanation of how the selections are alike and different. Provide evidence from both texts to support your ideas.

Writing to Sources Review both selections with students. Ask them to list similarities and differences in a Venn diagram. Suggest they begin by identifying the genre and purpose of each text. Tell students to use their Venn diagram to help them organize and support their ideas as they write their explanation.

Informative/Explanatory Writing Rubric					
Score	**Focus**	**Organization**	**Development of Evidence**	**Language and Vocabulary**	**Conventions**
4	Main idea is clearly conveyed and well supported; response is focused.	Organization is clear and effective, creating a sense of cohesion.	Evidence is relevant and thorough; includes facts and details.	Ideas are clearly and effectively conveyed, using precise language and/or domain-specific vocabulary.	Command of conventions is strongly demonstrated.
3	Main idea is clear, adequately supported; response is generally focused.	Organization is clear, though minor flaws may be present and some ideas may be disconnected.	Evidence is adequate and includes facts and details.	Ideas are adequately conveyed, using both precise and more general language; may include domain-specific vocabulary.	Command of conventions is sufficiently demonstrated.
2	Main idea is somewhat supported; lacks focus or includes unnecessary material.	Organization is inconsistent, and flaws are apparent.	Evidence is uneven or incomplete; insufficient use of facts and details.	Ideas are unevenly conveyed, using overly-simplistic language; lacks domain-specific vocabulary.	Command of conventions is uneven.
1	Response may be confusing, unfocused; main idea insufficiently supported.	Organization is poor or nonexistent.	Evidence is poor or nonexistent.	Ideas are conveyed in a vague, unclear, or confusing manner.	There is very little command of conventions.
0	The response shows no evidence of the ability to construct a coherent explanatory essay using information from sources.				

© Common Core State Standards

Writing 2. Write informative/explanatory texts to examine a topic and convey ideas and information clearly.

Write Like a Reporter
Informative/Explanatory Paragraph

Student Prompt Reread pp. 442–449 of *Talking Walls: Art for the People*. Which two murals are about education? Based on evidence from the text and illustrations, write a short report about each of the two murals. Include a description of the mural and an explanation of what it means.

_____

_____

_____

_____

_____

_____

_____

_____

_____

_____

_____

_____

_____

_____

_____

_____

Write Like a Reporter
Informative/Explanatory Paragraph

Student Prompt, p. 174 Reread pp. 442–449 of *Talking Walls: Art for the People.* Which two murals are about education? Based on evidence from the text and illustrations, write a short report about each of the two murals. Include a description of the mural and an explanation of what it means.

Writing to Sources Have students review the text to find the two murals that are about education. Tell them to take notes about what each mural looks like and the main idea of each mural. Point out that they can determine the main idea by looking at the details and title of the mural. Encourage students to use precise words in their description so readers can picture the murals clearly.

Students' reports should:
- describe and explain the meaning of each mural
- provide facts and details to develop the topic and support their ideas
- use precise words and phrases to clearly communicate ideas
- demonstrate strong command of the conventions of standard written English

---

© **Common Core State Standards**

Writing 2. Write informative/explanatory texts to examine a topic and convey ideas and information clearly.

Connect the Texts
Informative/Explanatory Comparison

Student Prompt Think about the selections *Talking Walls: Art for the People* and "The History of Palindromes." Write a short explanation that compares and contrasts the topics, genres, language, use of graphics, and purposes for writing the two texts. Use evidence from both texts to support your ideas.

_____

_____

_____

_____

_____

_____

_____

_____

_____

_____

_____

_____

_____

_____

_____

_____

_____

_____

Connect the Texts
Informative/Explanatory Comparison

Student Prompt, p. 176 Think about the selections *Talking Walls: Art for the People* and "The History of Palindromes." Write a short explanation that compares and contrasts the topics, genres, language, use of graphics, and purposes for writing the two texts. Use evidence from both texts to support your ideas.

Writing to Sources Review both texts with students. Have them make a T-chart and fill in their ideas about each of the topics below the correct selection title. Point out that this chart will help students gather details from the texts and organize their ideas before they begin writing their explanation.

	Informative/Explanatory Writing Rubric				
Score	**Focus**	**Organization**	**Development of Evidence**	**Language and Vocabulary**	**Conventions**
4	Main idea is clearly conveyed and well supported; response is focused.	Organization is clear and effective, creating a sense of cohesion.	Evidence is relevant and thorough; includes facts and details.	Ideas are clearly and effectively conveyed, using precise language and/or domain-specific vocabulary.	Command of conventions is strongly demonstrated.
3	Main idea is clear, adequately supported; response is generally focused.	Organization is clear, though minor flaws may be present and some ideas may be disconnected.	Evidence is adequate and includes facts and details.	Ideas are adequately conveyed, using both precise and more general language; may include domain-specific vocabulary.	Command of conventions is sufficiently demonstrated.
2	Main idea is somewhat supported; lacks focus or includes unnecessary material.	Organization is inconsistent, and flaws are apparent.	Evidence is uneven or incomplete; insufficient use of facts and details.	Ideas are unevenly conveyed, using overly-simplistic language; lacks domain-specific vocabulary.	Command of conventions is uneven.
1	Response may be confusing, unfocused; main idea insufficiently supported.	Organization is poor or nonexistent.	Evidence is poor or nonexistent.	Ideas are conveyed in a vague, unclear, or confusing manner.	There is very little command of conventions.
0	The response shows no evidence of the ability to construct a coherent explanatory essay using information from sources.				

Ⓒ **Common Core State Standards**

Writing 2. Write informative/explanatory texts to examine a topic and convey ideas and information clearly.

Write Like a Reporter
Informative/Explanatory Paragraph

Student Prompt Reread pp. 476–485 of *Two Bad Ants*. Write an explanation of what happens to the two ants after they decide to stay behind. First describe the events as the ants interpret them and then explain what really happens to the ants. Use evidence from the text and the illustrations to support your ideas.

_____

_____

_____

_____

_____

_____

_____

_____

_____

_____

_____

_____

_____

_____

_____

_____

Write Like a Reporter
Informative/Explanatory Paragraph

Student Prompt, p. 178 Reread pp. 476–485 of *Two Bad Ants*. Write an explanation of what happens to the two ants after they decide to stay behind. First describe the events as the ants interpret them and then explain what really happens to the ants. Use evidence from the text and the illustrations to support your ideas.

Writing to Sources Have students fill in a T-chart with what the ants think is happening in one column and what is actually happening in the other column. Tell students they can use this chart to help organize their ideas as they write their explanation. Remind students to look in both the text and the illustrations for evidence to support their ideas.

Students' explanations should:

- give a description of the ants' interpretation of the events
- tell what actually happens to the two ants
- provide details to develop the topic and support their ideas
- demonstrate strong command of the conventions of standard written English

Writing 2. Write informative/explanatory texts to examine a topic and convey ideas and information clearly.

Connect the Texts
Informative/Explanatory Paragraph

Student Prompt Reread the story *Two Bad Ants*. Think about the problems the ants face inside. Which of those problems can be problems for people as well? Then reread "Hiking Safety Tips" and think about the problems people can face outside. Write an explanation of the problems people can face both inside and outside; include ways to stay safe. Use text evidence to support your ideas.

_____

_____

_____

_____

_____

_____

_____

_____

_____

_____

_____

_____

_____

_____

Connect the Texts
Informative/Explanatory Paragraph

Student Prompt, p. 180 Reread the story *Two Bad Ants*. Think about the problems the ants face inside. Which of those problems can be problems for people as well? Then reread "Hiking Safety Tips" and think about the problems people can face outside. Write an explanation of the problems people can face both inside and outside; include ways to stay safe. Use text evidence to support your ideas.

Writing to Sources Have students return to both texts and find and list problems people can face inside and outside. Explain that students can use the illustrations as well as the text to identify problems people face. Then have students list ways people can stay safe inside and outside using evidence from the texts and their own experiences. Have students use their lists to organize and support their ideas as they write their explanation.

Informative/Explanatory Writing Rubric					
Score	Focus	Organization	Development of Evidence	Language and Vocabulary	Conventions
4	Main idea is clearly conveyed and well supported; response is focused.	Organization is clear and effective, creating a sense of cohesion.	Evidence is relevant and thorough; includes facts and details.	Ideas are clearly and effectively conveyed, using precise language and/or domain-specific vocabulary.	Command of conventions is strongly demonstrated.
3	Main idea is clear, adequately supported; response is generally focused.	Organization is clear, though minor flaws may be present and some ideas may be disconnected.	Evidence is adequate and includes facts and details.	Ideas are adequately conveyed, using both precise and more general language; may include domain-specific vocabulary.	Command of conventions is sufficiently demonstrated.
2	Main idea is somewhat supported; lacks focus or includes unnecessary material.	Organization is inconsistent, and flaws are apparent.	Evidence is uneven or incomplete; insufficient use of facts and details.	Ideas are unevenly conveyed, using overly-simplistic language; lacks domain-specific vocabulary.	Command of conventions is uneven.
1	Response may be confusing, unfocused; main idea insufficiently supported.	Organization is poor or nonexistent.	Evidence is poor or nonexistent.	Ideas are conveyed in a vague, unclear, or confusing manner.	There is very little command of conventions.
0	The response shows no evidence of the ability to construct a coherent explanatory essay using information from sources.				

© Common Core State Standards

Writing 2. Write informative/explanatory texts to examine a topic and convey ideas and information clearly.

Write Like a Reporter
Informative/Explanatory Paragraph

Student Prompt Reread pp. 512–519 of *Atlantis: The Legend of a Lost City*. Write a summary of the story in your own words. Include an explanation of how the story illustrates the theme stated in the last paragraph. Use text evidence to support your ideas.

_____

_____

_____

_____

_____

_____

_____

_____

_____

_____

_____

_____

_____

_____

_____

_____

Write Like a Reporter

Informative/Explanatory Paragraph

> **Student Prompt, p. 182** Reread pp. 512–519 of *Atlantis: The Legend of a Lost City*. Write a summary of the story in your own words. Include an explanation of how the story illustrates the theme stated in the last paragraph. Use text evidence to support your ideas.

Writing to Sources Remind students that when they write a summary, they tell about the most important events or ideas in their own words. Have them take notes about important events and ideas as they reread the text. Tell students that they can use these notes as they write their summary and explain how the selection illustrates the stated theme. Encourage students to use words and phrases such as *because*, *and*, and *but* to connect their ideas.

Students' paragraphs should:

- include a summary of major events and ideas in the story
- tell how the story illustrates the stated theme
- connect ideas using linking words and phrases such as *because*, *and*, and *but*
- demonstrate strong command of the conventions of standard written English

Ⓒ **Common Core State Standards**

Writing 2. Write informative/explanatory texts to examine a topic and convey ideas and information clearly.

Atlantis • Unit 6 • Week 5   **183**

Connect the Texts
Informative/Explanatory Essay

Student Prompt Look back at *Atlantis: The Legend of a Lost City* and "The Monster in the Maze." How are the two selections alike? How are they different? Write an essay that compares and contrasts their structures, characters, settings, plots, and themes. Use text evidence to support your ideas.

_____

_____

_____

_____

_____

_____

_____

_____

_____

_____

_____

_____

_____

_____

_____

_____

_____

Connect the Texts
Informative/Explanatory Essay

Student Prompt, p. 184 Look back at *Atlantis: The Legend of a Lost City* and "The Monster in the Maze." How are the two selections alike? How are they different? Write an essay that compares and contrasts their structures, characters, settings, plots, and themes. Use text evidence to support your ideas.

Writing to Sources Review both texts with students. Have them make a Venn diagram and write ways the two selections are similar and different. As students write their essays, they should use information from the Venn diagram as evidence to support their ideas. Remind students to begin their essay by introducing the topic and to end with a concluding statement.

Informative/Explanatory Writing Rubric					
Score	**Focus**	**Organization**	**Development of Evidence**	**Language and Vocabulary**	**Conventions**
4	Main idea is clearly conveyed and well supported; response is focused.	Organization is clear and effective, creating a sense of cohesion.	Evidence is relevant and thorough; includes facts and details.	Ideas are clearly and effectively conveyed, using precise language and/or domain-specific vocabulary.	Command of conventions is strongly demonstrated.
3	Main idea is clear, adequately supported; response is generally focused.	Organization is clear, though minor flaws may be present and some ideas may be disconnected.	Evidence is adequate and includes facts and details.	Ideas are adequately conveyed, using both precise and more general language; may include domain-specific vocabulary.	Command of conventions is sufficiently demonstrated.
2	Main idea is somewhat supported; lacks focus or includes unnecessary material.	Organization is inconsistent, and flaws are apparent.	Evidence is uneven or incomplete; insufficient use of facts and details.	Ideas are unevenly conveyed, using overly-simplistic language; lacks domain-specific vocabulary.	Command of conventions is uneven.
1	Response may be confusing, unfocused; main idea insufficiently supported.	Organization is poor or nonexistent.	Evidence is poor or nonexistent.	Ideas are conveyed in a vague, unclear, or confusing manner.	There is very little command of conventions.
0	The response shows no evidence of the ability to construct a coherent explanatory essay using information from sources.				

© Common Core State Standards

Writing 2. Write informative/explanatory texts to examine a topic and convey ideas and information clearly.

Prove It!
Informative/Explanatory Essay

Works of Art

Informative/Explanatory Compare and Contrast Essay

In this unit, students have read examples of informative/explanatory writing, including narrative nonfiction and expository text, and have had the opportunity to write in this mode. Remind students of texts and writing tasks (such as Write Like a Reporter and Connect the Texts) in which they have encountered and practiced informative/explanatory writing.

Key Features of a Compare and Contrast Essay

- explains the similarities and differences between people, places, or things
- uses specific details, facts, and examples to compare and contrast
- uses words that express similarities and differences
- provides a concluding statement or section summarizing similarities and differences

Writing Task Overview

Each unit writing task provides students with an opportunity to write to sources. To successfully complete the task, students must analyze, synthesize, and evaluate multiple complex texts and create their own written response.

Works of Art

Part 1: Students will reread and take notes on the selected sources. They will then respond to several questions about these sources and discuss their written responses with partners or in small groups.

Part 2: Students will work individually to plan, write, and revise their own compare and contrast essay.

Scorable Products: evidence-based short responses, compare and contrast essay

Works of Art: Writing Task – Short Response

Teacher Directions:

1. **Introduce the Sources** Refer students to the following texts in the Student Edition:

   1. *The Story of the Statue of Liberty*, pp. 374–385

   2. *Happy Birthday Mr. Kang*, pp. 402–419

   3. *Talking Walls: Art for the People*, pp. 438–451

   Explain to students that they will need to draw evidence and support from the texts above in order to answer evidence-based short response questions and to write a compare and contrast essay. Students should take notes and categorize information as they closely reread the texts. Students should be given paper or a relevant graphic organizer from the TR DVD for note-taking.

2. **Provide Student Directions and Scoring Information (p. 190)** Answer any task-related questions students may have. If necessary, provide additional paper for students to write their responses.

3. **Initiate the Writing Task** If you are timing this part of the task, you may wish to alert students when half the allotted time has elapsed and again when 5 minutes remain.

4. **Facilitate Collaboration** After students have completed their written responses to the evidence-based short response questions, assign partners or small groups and have them discuss their responses. If students struggle to work together productively, provide them with tips and strategies for expressing their ideas and building on others'.

Ⓒ **Common Core State Standards**

Writing 2. Write informative/explanatory texts to examine a topic and convey ideas and information clearly.

Unit 6 **187**

Scoring Information

Use the following 2-point scoring rubrics to evaluate students' answers to the evidence-based short response questions.

1. Compare the works of art described in the three stories. How are the works of art similar and different?

	Analysis Rubric	
2	The response: • demonstrates the ability to analyze similarities and differences in works of art among the texts • includes specific details that make reference to the texts	
1	The response: • demonstrates a limited ability to analyze similarities and differences in works of art among the texts • includes some details that make reference to the texts	
0	A response receives no credit if it demonstrates no ability to analyze similarities and differences in works of art among the texts or includes no relevant details from the texts.	

2. What connection does each work of art have to immigrants or immigration? Give examples from the texts to support your answer.

	Synthesis Rubric	
2	The response: • demonstrates the ability to synthesize information from the sources in order to make sound connections • includes specific details that make reference to the texts	
1	The response: • demonstrates a limited ability to synthesize information from the sources in order to make sound connections • includes some details that make reference to the texts	
0	A response receives no credit if it demonstrates no ability to synthesize information from the sources in order to make sound connections.	

3. Which of the works of art described in the texts is most meaningful to you? Why? Cite examples from the text.

	Evaluation Rubric
2	The response: • demonstrates the ability to evaluate texts in order to identify meaning in art and explain what makes it meaningful • includes specific details that make reference to the texts
1	The response: • demonstrates a limited ability to evaluate texts in order to identify meaning in art and explain what makes it meaningful • includes some details that make reference to the texts
0	A response receives no credit if it demonstrates no ability to evaluate texts or includes no relevant details from the texts.

Ⓒ **Common Core State Standards**

Writing 9. Draw evidence from literary or informational texts to support analysis, reflection, and research.

Works of Art
Writing Task – Short Response

Student Directions:

Your Assignment You will reread several selections from Unit 6 and take notes on these sources. Then you will answer three questions about these materials. You may refer to your notes or to any of the sources as often as you like.

Sources
1. *The Story of the Statue of Liberty,* pp. 374–385

2. *Happy Birthday Mr. Kang,* pp. 402–419

3. *Talking Walls: Art for the People,* pp. 438–451

Be sure to read closely and take good notes. Your sources and notes will be the basis for writing your own compare and contrast essay in the second half of this writing task.

Evidence-Based Short Response Questions Answer the short response questions on the lines provided below each question. Your answers to these questions will be scored. Be sure to base your answers on the sources you have just read. Remember that you may refer back to your notes or to any of the sources.

After you have answered the questions, you will discuss your responses with a partner or in a small group. Your teacher will let you know when to begin the discussion part of this task.

Scoring Information Your responses will be scored based on how you demonstrate the ability to:

- compare information about works of art across texts
- include specific details that clearly reference the sources
- locate and use information from the sources
- evaluate meaningful information

Name _____

Evidence-Based Short Response Questions

1. Compare the works of art described in the three stories. How are the works of art similar and different?

_____

_____

_____

_____

2. What connection does each work of art have to immigrants or immigration? Give examples from the texts to support your answer.

_____

_____

_____

_____

3. Which of the works of art described in the texts is most meaningful to you? Why? Cite examples from the texts.

_____

_____

_____

_____

Collaborative Discussion

After you have written your responses to the questions, discuss your ideas. Your teacher will assign you a partner or a small group and let you know when to begin.

Works of Art: Writing Task – Compare and Contrast Essay

Teacher Directions:

1. **Provide Student Directions and Scoring Information (p. 194)** Explain to students that they will now review their notes and sources and plan, draft, and revise their compare and contrast essays. Although they may use their notes and sources, they must work alone. Students will be allowed to look back at the answers they wrote to the short response questions, but they are not allowed to make changes to those answers. Have students read the directions for the compare and contrast essay and answer any task-related questions they may have. Students should be given paper on which to write their compare and contrast essay.

2. **Initiate the Writing Task** If you are timing this part of the task, you may wish to suggest approximate times for students to begin writing and revising. If students wish to continue writing rather than revising, allow them to do so. Alert students when 5 minutes remain.

3. **Scoring Information** Use the scoring rubric on the next page to evaluate students' compare and contrast essays.

4. **Compare and Contrast Essay Prompt** Use what you have learned from reading *The Story of the Statue of Liberty, Happy Birthday Mr. Kang*, and *Talking Walls: Art for the People* to write a compare and contrast essay about two works of art that inspire you and others. Use facts, details, and personal examples to tell how the works of art are alike and different. Use details from the selections to help illustrate how art inspires people. Be sure to follow the conventions of written English.

Informative/Explanatory Writing Rubric

Score	Focus	Organization	Development of Evidence	Language and Vocabulary	Conventions
4	Main idea is carefully conveyed and well supported with evidence; response is focused.	Organization is clear and effective, creating a sense of structure.	Evidence is relevant and thorough; includes facts and details.	Ideas are clearly and effectively stated, using precise language with domain-specific vocabulary.	Command of conventions is strongly demonstrated.
3	Main idea is conveyed and adequately supported with evidence; response is generally focused.	Organization is clear; minor flaws may be present and some ideas may be disconnected.	Evidence is adequate and includes some facts and details.	Ideas are adequately stated, using more general language; may include domain-specific vocabulary.	Command of conventions is sufficiently demonstrated.
2	Main idea is somewhat supported; lacks focus by including unnecessary material.	Organization is inconsistent with major flaws.	Evidence is incomplete with insufficient use of facts or details.	Ideas are unevenly stated, using overly-simplistic language; lacks domain-specific vocabulary.	Command of conventions is uneven.
1	Response may be confusing, unfocused; main idea insufficiently supported.	Organization is poor or nonexistent.	Evidence is poor or nonexistent.	Ideas are conveyed in a vague or confusing manner.	There is very little command of conventions.
0	The response shows no evidence of the ability to construct a coherent informative/explanatory essay using information from sources.				

Common Core State Standards

Writing 2. Write informative/explanatory texts to examine a topic and convey ideas and information clearly. **Writing 2.a.** Introduce a topic and group related information together. **Writing 2.b.** Develop the topic with facts, definitions, and details. **Writing 9.** Draw evidence from literary or informational texts to support analysis, reflection, and research. **Writing 10.** Write routinely over extended time frames (time for research, reflection, and revision) and shorter time frames (a single sitting or a day or two) for a range of discipline-specific tasks, purposes, and audiences.

Works of Art
Writing Task – Compare and Contrast Essay

Student Directions:

Your Assignment Now you will review your notes and sources and plan, draft, and revise your compare and contrast essay. While you may use your notes and refer to your sources, you must work on your own. You may also refer to the answers you wrote to earlier questions, but you cannot change those answers.

Compare and Contrast Essay Prompt Use what you have learned from reading *The Story of the Statue of Liberty, Happy Birthday Mr. Kang,* and *Talking Walls: Art for the People* to write a compare and contrast essay about two works of art that inspire you and others. Use facts, details, and personal examples to tell how the works of art are alike and different. Use details from the selections to help illustrate how art inspires people. Be sure to follow the conventions of written English.

Scoring Information Your compare and contrast essay will be assigned a score for

1. **Focus** – how well you maintain your focus on the topics
2. **Organization** – how well you organize a comparison
3. **Development** – how well you develop the essay with details
4. **Language and Vocabulary** – how well you develop the essay using precise language and domain-specific vocabulary
5. **Conventions** – how well you follow the rules of usage, punctuation, capitalization, and spelling

Now begin work on your compare and contrast essay. Try to manage your time carefully so that you can

- plan your compare and contrast essay
- write your compare and contrast essay
- revise and edit for a final draft

Works of Art: Writing Task – Compare and Contrast Essay

Teacher Directions:

1. Publish Explain to students that publishing their writing is the last step in the writing process. If time permits, have students review one another's essays and incorporate any comments their classmates have. Discuss different ways technology can be used to publish writing.

2. Present Students will now have the option to present their compare and contrast essays. Have students give speeches about their compare and contrast essays in front of the class. Use the list below to offer students tips on listening and speaking.

While Listening to a Classmate...

- Face the speaker to listen attentively.
- Take notes on what the speaker says.

While Speaking to Classmates...

- Determine your purpose for speaking.
- Have good posture and eye contact.
- Speak at an appropriate pace.

Things to Do Together...

- Ask and answer questions with detail.
- Build on each other's ideas.

More Connect the Texts

Opinion Paragraph

Objectives

- Identify the characteristics of an opinion paragraph.
- Write an opinion paragraph, using facts and supporting details.
- Evaluate your writing.
- Revise and publish your writing.

Ⓒ Common Core State Standards

Writing 1. Write opinion pieces on topics or texts, supporting a point of view with reasons. **Writing 1.a.** Introduce the topic or text they are writing about, state an opinion, and create an organizational structure that lists reasons. **Writing 1.b.** Provide reasons that support the opinion. **Writing 1.c.** Use linking words and phrases (e.g., *because, therefore, since, for example*) to connect opinion and reasons. **Writing 1.d.** Provide a concluding statement or section.

STEP 1 Read Like a Writer

Review the key features of an opinion paragraph listed below. Respond to any questions students might have.

Key Features of an Opinion Paragraph

- Introduces the topic and states the writer's opinion about the topic
- Supports the opinion with reasons
- Organizes reasons using a structure such as order of importance
- Uses linking words and phrases to connect the opinion and reasons
- Uses persuasive words to make writing more convincing
- Provides a concluding statement or section

Choose an opinion piece or persuasive text that students have already read to model key features. Display the model for students to see and point out each of the key features you have discussed.

STEP 2 Organize Your Ideas

Writing Prompt Look back at *What About Me?* and "How the Desert Tortoise Got Its Shell." What role does working together, or cooperation, play in the stories? Write an opinion paragraph on this topic: "When you are working with others, nothing is more important than cooperation." Do you agree or disagree? State your opinion and then support it with evidence from both texts.

Think Aloud Your ideas will be more persuasive if they are well organized and clearly presented. First decide what opinion, or claim, you will state in your paragraph. Then choose the reasons, facts, details, and examples from the texts that you will use to support your opinion. You may wish to make an outline.

Guided Writing Display a simple outline. Explain to students that when they write their paragraph, they will first state their opinion, then tell about their reasons in a logical order, and end with a statement that sums up their opinion and reasons.

STEP 3 Draft Your Writing

Have students use their outlines to write an opinion paragraph. Remind them of the key features of an opinion paragraph.

Think Aloud The best way to persuade readers to agree with your opinion is to support it with enough facts and details. Gather details and examples from the texts *What About Me?* and "How the Desert Tortoise Got Its Shell." Think of examples from your own or others' experiences. You can also look through books, articles, and Web sites to find additional information.

Getting Started Tell students to begin writing their opinion paragraph using their outlines to keep them focused on the topic. Give them suggestions on how to organize their reasons, facts, and details in ways that make sense. Brainstorm linking words and phrases, such as *because* and *for example,* and persuasive words, such as *best* and *worst,* that they can use in their writing. Emphasize the importance of using correct grammar and complete sentences. Remind students to end their opinion paragraph with a concluding statement that restates their opinion and reasons for readers to remember.

STEP 4 Evaluate Your Writing

Display the checklist below and have students use it to evaluate their opinion paragraphs. Circulate around the room and confer with individual students.

- ✓ Did I introduce my topic at the beginning?
- ✓ Did I state my opinion clearly?
- ✓ Do my reasons support my opinion?
- ✓ Did I list my reasons using a structure that makes sense?
- ✓ Did I use linking words to connect my opinion and reasons and persuasive words to make my writing more convincing?
- ✓ Does my concluding statement sum up my opinion and reasons?

Help students set goals and make a plan for improving in areas where their writing needs help.

STEP 5 Revise and Publish

Help students follow through with their plans for revision. If time permits, have students trade opinion paragraphs and offer one another suggestions for how to improve the writing.

Publishing Students can publish their opinion paragraphs by posting them on a bulletin board for classmates and others to read.

More Connect the Texts
Character Review

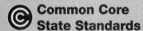
STEP 1 Read Like a Writer

Review the key features of a character review listed below. Respond to any questions students might have.

Key Features of a Character Review

- Introduces the topic and states the writer's opinion about the topic
- Supports the opinion with reasons
- Supports the reasons with facts and details from the texts
- Organizes reasons using a structure such as similarities and differences
- Uses linking words and phrases to connect the opinion and reasons
- Provides a concluding statement or section

Choose an opinion piece or persuasive text that students have already read to model key features. Display the model for students to see and point out each of the key features you have discussed.

STEP 2 Organize Your Ideas

Writing Prompt Look back at *What About Me?* and *My Rows and Piles of Coins.* The main characters in both stories set goals for themselves and then work hard to achieve those goals. Write a review that tells which character you admire more and why. State your opinion and then support it with evidence from both texts.

Think Aloud Your writing will be more persuasive if you organize and present your ideas clearly. First decide what opinion you will state in your review and what the reasons for your opinion will be. Then choose facts, details, and examples from the texts that you will use to support your reasons. Review each text and make a list before you begin writing.

Guided Writing Show students how to make a list of relevant information. Write the name of the character followed by details of the character's actions, thoughts, and feelings that reveal what the character is like. Explain to students that when they write their review, they will begin by briefly describing and comparing the two characters. Then they will state their opinion, tell about their reasons in a logical order, and end with a statement that sums up their opinion and reasons.

STEP 3 Draft Your Writing

Have students use their lists to write a character review. Remind them of the key features of a character review.

Think Aloud How can you persuade readers to agree with your opinion? Give them reasons, facts, and details that clearly support your opinion. Make lists of details about the main characters in *What About Me?* and *My Rows and Piles of Coins.*

Getting Started Tell students to begin writing their character review using their lists to help them stay on topic. Offer suggestions about organizing their reasons, facts, and details in logical ways. Brainstorm linking words and phrases, such as *because* and *for example,* that they can use to connect their opinion and reasons. Emphasize the importance of using correct grammar and complete sentences. Remind students to end their character review with a concluding statement that restates their opinion and reasons for readers to remember.

STEP 4 Evaluate Your Writing

Display the checklist below and have students use it to evaluate their character reviews. Circulate around the room and confer with individual students.

✓ Did I introduce my topic at the beginning?

✓ Did I state my opinion clearly?

✓ Do my reasons support my opinion?

✓ Did I use text evidence to support my reasons?

✓ Did I list my reasons using a structure that makes sense?

✓ Did I use linking words to connect my opinion and reasons?

✓ Does my concluding statement sum up my opinion and reasons?

Help students set goals and make a plan for improving in areas where their writing needs help.

STEP 5 Revise and Publish

Help students follow through with their plans for revision. If time permits, have students trade character reviews and offer suggestions for how to improve the writing.

Publishing Students can publish their character reviews by sharing them with family members.

Opinion Paragraph

Objectives

- Identify the characteristics of an opinion paragraph.
- Write an opinion paragraph, using facts and supporting details.
- Evaluate your writing.
- Revise and publish your writing.

Common Core State Standards

Writing 1. Write opinion pieces on topics or texts, supporting a point of view with reasons. **Writing 1.a.** Introduce the topic or text they are writing about, state an opinion, and create an organizational structure that lists reasons. **Writing 1.b.** Provide reasons that support the opinion. **Writing 1.c.** Use linking words and phrases (e.g., *because, therefore, since, for example*) to connect opinion and reasons. **Writing 1.d.** Provide a concluding statement or section.

STEP 1 Read Like a Writer

Review the key features of an opinion paragraph listed below. Respond to any questions students might have.

Key Features of an Opinion Paragraph

- Introduces the topic and states the writer's opinion about the topic
- Supports the opinion with reasons
- Organizes reasons using a structure such as order of importance
- Uses linking words and phrases to connect the opinion and reasons
- Uses persuasive words to make writing more convincing
- Provides a concluding statement or section

Choose an opinion piece or persuasive text that students have already read to model key features. Display the model for students to see and point out each of the key features you have discussed.

STEP 2 Organize Your Ideas

Writing Prompt Look back at *I Wanna Iguana* and *Prudy's Problem and How She Solved It.* Both stories tell about a child who has a problem and how that child solves the problem. Of the two solutions, which do you think is better? Write an opinion paragraph that answers this question. State your opinion and then support it with evidence from both texts.

Think Aloud Your ideas will be more persuasive if they are well organized and clearly presented. First decide what opinion you will state in your paragraph. Then choose the reasons, facts, details, and examples from the texts that you will use to support your opinion. You may wish to make a chart before you begin writing.

Guided Writing Display a two-column chart. Demonstrate writing the characters' names as column headings and details about their problem and solution in the columns. Explain to students that when they write their paragraphs, they will first state their opinion, then tell about their reasons in a logical order, and end with a statement that sums up their opinion and reasons.

STEP 3 Draft Your Writing

Have students use their charts to write an opinion paragraph. Remind them of the key features of an opinion paragraph.

Think Aloud The best way to persuade readers to agree with your opinion is to support it with enough text evidence. Gather details and examples from *I Wanna Iguana* and *Prudy's Problem and How She Solved It.* Think of examples from your own or others' experiences.

Getting Started Tell students to begin writing their opinion paragraphs using their charts to keep them focused on the topic. Give them suggestions on how to organize their reasons, facts, and details in ways that make sense. Brainstorm linking words and phrases, such as *because* and *for example,* and persuasive words, such as *good* and *should,* that students can use in their writing. Emphasize the importance of using correct grammar and complete sentences. Remind students to end their opinion paragraph with a concluding statement that restates their opinion and reasons for readers to remember.

STEP 4 Evaluate Your Writing

Display the checklist below and have students use it to evaluate their opinion paragraphs. Circulate around the room and confer with individual students.

✓ Did I introduce my topic at the beginning?

✓ Did I state my opinion clearly?

✓ Do my reasons support my opinion?

✓ Did I list my reasons using a structure that makes sense?

✓ Did I use linking words to connect my opinion and reasons and persuasive words to make my writing more convincing?

✓ Does my concluding statement sum up my opinion and reasons?

Help students set goals and make a plan for improving in areas where their writing needs help.

STEP 5 Revise and Publish

Help students follow through with their plans for revision. If time permits, have students trade opinion paragraphs and offer one another suggestions for how to improve the writing.

Publishing Students can publish their opinion paragraphs by posting them on a class blog for classmates and others to read.

More Connect the Texts
Advertisement

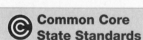
STEP 1 Read Like a Writer

Review the key features of an advertisement listed below. Respond to any questions students might have.

Key Features of an Advertisement

- States the writer's opinion, or claim
- Supports the claim with facts, details, and examples
- Organizes the information in an easy-to-read format
- Uses persuasive words to make the claim more convincing
- Includes graphics such as photographs or illustrations
- Provides a concluding statement or section

Bring in an advertisement to model key features. Display the model for students to see and point out each of the key features you have discussed.

STEP 2 Organize Your Ideas

Writing Prompt Look back at *Prudy's Problem and How She Solved It* and "Meeting the Challenge of Collecting." Both selections describe museums that people can visit. Write an advertisement for these two museums. Persuade people that they should visit both museums. Provide evidence from both texts to support your opinion, or claim.

Think Aloud Your writing will be more persuasive if you organize and present your ideas clearly. First decide how you will state your claim in a way that draws readers into your advertisement. Then choose the facts, details, and examples from the selections that you will use to support your claim. Review each selection and make a list before you begin writing.

Guided Writing Show students how to make lists of relevant information. Write the name of the museum and details about it from the selection's text and illustrations. Explain to students that when they write their advertisements, they will begin by briefly describing the museums. Then they will state their claim; present their supporting facts, details, and examples in a way that will appeal to readers; and end with a statement that sums up why people should visit the museums.

STEP 3 Draft Your Writing

Have students use their lists to write an advertisement. Remind them of the key features of an advertisement.

Think Aloud How can you persuade readers to visit the museums? Give them facts, details, and examples that will make them want to go to those places. Make lists of details about the museums in *Prudy's Problem and How She Solved It* and "Meeting the Challenge of Collecting." You can also list details and ideas from your own experiences and from your imagination.

Getting Started Tell students to begin writing their advertisements using their lists to help them. Discuss how they can organize their facts and details in a way that is easy to read and understand. Brainstorm persuasive words, such as *great, important, should, need,* and *everyone,* that they can use to make their writing more convincing. Emphasize the importance of using correct grammar and complete sentences. Remind students to end their advertisements with a concluding statement or section that sums up what they want readers to do and why. Suggest that they include graphics, such as illustrations, and design elements, such as different font sizes, to help their advertisement catch a reader's eye.

STEP 4 Evaluate Your Writing

Display the checklist below and have students use it to evaluate their advertisements. Circulate around the room and confer with individual students.

✓ Did I state my opinion, or claim, clearly?

✓ Do the facts, details, and examples support my claim?

✓ Is the information organized in an easy-to-read format?

✓ Did I use persuasive words to make my claim more convincing?

✓ Did I use graphics that help support the text?

✓ Does my concluding statement or section sum up my claim and evidence?

Help students set goals and make a plan for improving in areas where their writing needs help.

STEP 5 Revise and Publish

Help students follow through with their plans for revision. If time permits, have students trade advertisements and offer suggestions for how to improve the writing and layout.

Publishing Students can publish their advertisements by printing them out and distributing them to classmates, friends, and family members.

More Connect the Texts
Letter to the Editor

STEP 1 Read Like a Writer

Review the key features of a letter to the editor listed below. Respond to any questions students might have.

Key Features of a Letter to the Editor
- States the issue and the writer's point of view about the issue
- Supports the point of view with reasons, facts, and examples
- Organizes reasons using a structure such as order of importance
- Uses persuasive words to appeal to readers' beliefs and emotions
- Provides a concluding statement or section
- Uses the correct format for a letter

Choose a letter to the editor that students have already read to model key features. Display the model for students to see and point out each of the key features.

STEP 2 Organize Your Ideas

Writing Prompt Look back at *Penguin Chick* and *Amazing Bird Nests*. Write a letter to the editor on this issue: "People can learn a lot from birds." Do you agree or disagree? State your point of view and then support it with evidence from both texts.

Think Aloud Your letter to the editor will better persuade readers if your ideas are well organized and clearly presented. First decide which point of view you choose. Do you think people can learn a lot from birds or not? Then look for reasons, facts, and examples in the texts that you can use to support your point of view.

Guided Writing Display a simple outline. Show students where to write their point of view, reasons, and evidence. Explain that when they write their letter to the editor, they will first state their point of view on the issue, present their reasons in a logical order, and end with a statement that restates their point of view and reasons.

STEP 3 Draft Your Writing

Have students use their outlines to write a letter to the editor. Remind them of the key features of a letter to the editor.

Think Aloud The best way to persuade readers to agree with your point of view on an issue is to offer strong reasons and support them with valid facts and details. Gather appropriate information from the texts *Penguin Chick* and *Amazing Bird Nests.* You can also look through books, articles, and Web sites to find additional supporting information.

Getting Started Tell students to begin writing their letters to the editor using their outlines to help them. Brainstorm persuasive words, such as *best, worst, always, never, fair, unfair, need, should,* and *important,* that they can use in their writing. Tell students to end their letters to the editor with a concluding statement or section that restates their point of view and reasons so that readers will remember them. Emphasize the importance of using correct grammar and complete sentences. Remind students that they should use the correct format for a letter, which includes the date, a greeting, a closing, and a signature.

STEP 4 Evaluate Your Writing

Display the checklist below and have students use it to evaluate their letters to the editor. Circulate around the room and confer with individual students.

- ✓ Did I state my point of view on the issue clearly?
- ✓ Do my reasons, facts, and examples support my point of view?
- ✓ Did I use persuasive words to appeal to readers?
- ✓ Does my concluding statement or section restate my point of view and reasons?
- ✓ Did I use the correct format for a letter?

Help students set goals and make a plan for improving their writing.

STEP 5 Revise and Publish

Help students follow through with their plans for revision. If time permits, have students trade letters to the editor and offer one another suggestions for how to improve the writing.

Publishing Students can publish their letters to the editor by submitting them to the school newspaper or to a community publication.

More Connect the Texts
Opinion Paragraph

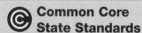
STEP 1 Read Like a Writer

Review the key features of an opinion paragraph listed below. Respond to any questions students might have.

Key Features of an Opinion Paragraph

- Introduces the topic and states the writer's opinion about the topic
- Supports the opinion with reasons
- Organizes reasons using a structure such as order of importance
- Uses linking words and phrases to connect the opinion and reasons
- Uses persuasive words to make writing more convincing
- Provides a concluding statement or section

Choose an opinion paragraph that students have already read to model key features. Display the model for students to see and point out each of the key features you have discussed.

STEP 2 Organize Your Ideas

Writing Prompt Look back at *How Do You Raise a Raisin?* and *Seeing Stars.* These selections are both expository text, but they are not organized the same way. Write an opinion paragraph that answers this question: How should expository text be organized? State your opinion and then support it with evidence from both selections.

Think Aloud Your ideas will be more persuasive if they are well organized and clearly presented. First decide what opinion you will state in your paragraph. Then choose the reasons, facts, details, and examples from the texts that you will use to support your opinion. You may wish to make a chart before you begin writing.

Guided Writing Display a two-column chart. Demonstrate writing the selection titles as column headings and details about their organization in the columns. Explain to students that when they write their paragraphs, they will begin by briefly describing the organization of each selection. Then they will state their opinion, tell about their reasons in a logical order, and end with a statement that sums up their opinion and reasons.

STEP 3 Draft Your Writing

Have students use their charts to write an opinion paragraph. Remind them of the key features of an opinion paragraph.

Think Aloud The best way to persuade readers to agree with your opinion is to support it with enough text evidence. Gather details and examples from *How Do You Raise a Raisin?* and *Seeing Stars.*

Getting Started Tell students to begin writing their opinion paragraphs using their charts to help them. Give them suggestions about organizing their reasons, facts, and details in logical ways. Brainstorm linking words and phrases, such as *since* and *therefore,* and persuasive words, such as *most* and *better,* that they can use in their writing. Emphasize the importance of using correct grammar and complete sentences. Remind students to end their opinion paragraphs with a concluding statement that restates their opinion and reasons for readers to remember.

STEP 4 Evaluate Your Writing

Display the checklist below and have students use it to evaluate their opinion paragraphs. Circulate around the room and confer with individual students.

✓ Did I introduce my topic at the beginning?

✓ Did I state my opinion clearly?

✓ Do my reasons support my opinion?

✓ Did I list my reasons using a structure that makes sense?

✓ Did I use linking words to connect my opinion and reasons and persuasive words to make my writing more convincing?

✓ Does my concluding statement sum up my opinion and reasons?

Help students set goals and make a plan for improving in areas where their writing needs help.

STEP 5 Revise and Publish

Help students follow through with their plans for revision. If time permits, have students trade opinion paragraphs and offer one another suggestions for how to improve the writing.

Publishing Students can print their opinion paragraphs and then read them aloud and discuss them in small groups.

More Connect the Texts
Story Review

Objectives

- Identify the characteristics of a story review.
- Write a story review, using facts and supporting details.
- Evaluate your writing.
- Revise and publish your writing.

 Common Core State Standards

Writing 1. Write opinion pieces on topics or texts, supporting a point of view with reasons. **Writing 1.a.** Introduce the topic or text they are writing about, state an opinion, and create an organizational structure that lists reasons. **Writing 1.b.** Provide reasons that support the opinion. **Writing 1.c.** Use linking words and phrases (e.g., *because, therefore, since, for example*) to connect opinion and reasons. **Writing 1.d.** Provide a concluding statement or section.

STEP 1 Read Like a Writer

Review the key features of a story review listed below. Respond to any questions students might have.

Key Features of a Story Review

- Introduces the topic and states the writer's opinion about the topic
- Supports the opinion with reasons
- Supports the reasons with facts and details from the text
- Organizes reasons using a structure such as order of importance
- Uses linking words and phrases to connect the opinion and reasons
- Provides a concluding statement or section

Choose a review that students have already read to model key features. Display the model for students to see and point out each of the key features you have discussed.

STEP 2 Organize Your Ideas

Writing Prompt Look back at *Pushing Up the Sky* and *A Symphony of Whales*. Both stories are about people helping and working together. Write a review that tells which story you like better and why. State your opinion and then support it with evidence from both texts.

Think Aloud Your writing will be more persuasive if you organize and present your ideas clearly. First decide what opinion you will state in your review and what the reasons for your opinion will be. Then choose facts, details, and examples from the texts that you will use to support your reasons. Review each text and make a concept web before you begin writing.

Guided Writing Show students how to make a concept web. Write the title of each story in the center circle and details about the characters, setting, plot, and theme, grouped by story element, in the outer circles. Explain to students that when they write their reviews, they will begin by briefly summarizing the two stories. Then they will state their opinion, present their reasons in a logical order, and end with a statement that sums up their opinion and reasons.

STEP 3 Draft Your Writing

Have students use their concept webs to write a story review. Remind them of the key features of a story review.

Think Aloud How can you persuade readers to agree with your opinion? Give them reasons, facts, and details that clearly support your opinion. Make concept webs that show details about the story elements in *Pushing Up the Sky* and *A Symphony of Whales.*

Getting Started Tell students to begin writing their story review using their concept webs to help them stay on topic. Offer suggestions about organizing their reasons, facts, and details in logical ways. Brainstorm linking words and phrases, such as *because* and *for example,* that they can use to connect their opinion and reasons. Emphasize the importance of using correct grammar and complete sentences. Remind students to end their story review with a concluding statement that restates their opinion and reasons for readers to remember.

STEP 4 Evaluate Your Writing

Display the checklist below and have students use it to evaluate their story reviews. Circulate around the room and confer with individual students.

✓ Did I introduce my topic at the beginning?

✓ Did I state my opinion clearly?

✓ Do my reasons support my opinion?

✓ Did I use text evidence to support my reasons?

✓ Did I list my reasons using a structure that makes sense?

✓ Did I use linking words to connect my opinion and reasons?

✓ Does my concluding statement sum up my opinion and reasons?

Help students set goals and make a plan for improving in areas where their writing needs help.

STEP 5 Revise and Publish

Help students follow through with their plans for revision. If time permits, have students trade story reviews and offer suggestions for how to improve the writing.

Publishing Students can publish their story reviews by compiling them to make a literature review magazine either in print or online.

Travel Brochure

Common Core State Standards

Writing 1. Write opinion pieces on topics or texts, supporting a point of view with reasons. **Writing 1.a.** Introduce the topic or text they are writing about, state an opinion, and create an organizational structure that lists reasons. **Writing 1.b.** Provide reasons that support the opinion. **Writing 1.c.** Use linking words and phrases (e.g., *because, therefore, since, for example*) to connect opinion and reasons. **Writing 1.d.** Provide a concluding statement or section.

STEP 1 Read Like a Writer

Review the key features of a travel brochure listed below. Respond to any questions students might have.

Key Features of a Travel Brochure
- States the writer's opinion, or claim
- Supports the claim with facts, details, and examples
- Organizes the information in an easy-to-read format
- Uses persuasive words to make the claim more convincing
- Includes graphics such as photographs or illustrations
- Provides a concluding statement or section

Bring in a travel brochure or another opinion piece to model key features. Display the model for students to see and point out each of the key features you have discussed.

STEP 2 Organize Your Ideas

Writing Prompt Look back at *Hottest, Coldest, Highest, Deepest* and "Paul Bunyan and the Great Lakes." Both selections tell about places that people might enjoy visiting. Write a travel brochure that tries to persuade people to visit some of these places. Use evidence from both texts to support your opinion, or claim.

Think Aloud Your travel brochure will be more persuasive if you organize and present your ideas clearly. First decide how you will state your claim in a way that draws readers into your travel brochure. Then choose the facts, details, and examples from the selections that you will use to support your claim. Review each selection and make a list before you begin writing.

Guided Writing Show students how to make lists of relevant information. Write the name of each place and details about it from the selection's text and illustrations. Explain to students that when they write their travel brochure, they will begin by stating their claim. Then they will briefly describe each place and present the supporting facts, details, and examples in a way that will appeal to readers. They will end with a statement that sums up why people would enjoy visiting these places.

STEP 3 Draft Your Writing

Have students use their lists to write a travel brochure. Remind them of the key features of a travel brochure.

Think Aloud How can you persuade readers to visit the Great Lakes and other places? Give them facts, details, and examples that will make them want to go to those places. Make lists of details about the places in *Hottest, Coldest, Highest, Deepest* and "Paul Bunyan and the Great Lakes." You can also list facts, details, and examples from your own travel experiences and from books, articles, and Web sites.

Getting Started Tell students to begin writing their travel brochures using their lists to help them. Discuss how they can organize their facts and details in a way that is easy to read and understand. Brainstorm persuasive words, such as *beautiful, exciting, unique, fun,* and *great,* that they can use to make their writing more convincing. Emphasize the importance of using correct grammar and complete sentences. Remind students to end their travel brochure with a concluding statement or section that sums up what they want readers to do and why. Suggest that they include graphics, such as illustrations, and design elements, such as different font sizes, to make their travel brochure grab a reader's attention.

STEP 4 Evaluate Your Writing

Display the checklist below and have students use it to evaluate their travel brochures. Circulate around the room and confer with individual students.

✓ Did I state my opinion, or claim, clearly?

✓ Do the facts, details, and examples support my claim?

✓ Is the information organized in an easy-to-read format?

✓ Did I use persuasive words to make my claim more convincing?

✓ Did I use graphics that help support the text?

✓ Does my concluding statement or section sum up my claim and evidence?

Help students set goals and make a plan for improving in areas where their writing needs help.

STEP 5 Revise and Publish

Help students follow through with their plans for revision. If time permits, have students trade travel brochures and offer suggestions for how to improve the writing and layout.

Publishing Students can publish their travel brochures by printing them out and distributing them to classmates, friends, and family members.

More Connect the Texts
Opinion Essay

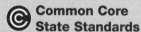
STEP 1 Read Like a Writer

Review the key features of an opinion essay listed below. Respond to any questions students might have.

Key Features of an Opinion Essay

- Introduces the topic and states the writer's opinion about the topic
- Supports the opinion with reasons
- Organizes reasons using a structure such as order of importance
- Uses linking words and phrases to connect the opinion and reasons
- Uses persuasive words to make writing more convincing
- Provides a concluding statement or section

Choose an opinion essay that students have already read to model key features. Display the model for students to see and point out each of the key features you have discussed.

STEP 2 Organize Your Ideas

Writing Prompt Look back at *Fly, Eagle, Fly!* and "Purple Coyote." Both texts are stories that teach a lesson. The lesson of the first story is "We all need to be true to our nature." The lesson of the second story is "Curiosity can cause trouble." Write an opinion essay that tells which lesson you think is more valuable and why. State your opinion and then support it with evidence from both selections.

Think Aloud Your ideas will be more persuasive if they are well organized and clearly presented. First decide what opinion you will state in your essay. Then choose the reasons, facts, details, and examples from the texts that you will use to support your opinion. You may wish to make a chart before you begin writing.

Guided Writing Display a two-column chart. Demonstrate writing each story title as a column heading and details about its characters, plot, and lesson in that column. Explain to students that when they write their essays, they will begin by briefly summarizing each story. Then they will state their opinion, present their reasons in a logical order, and end with a statement that sums up their opinion and reasons.

STEP 3 Draft Your Writing

Have students use their charts to write an opinion essay. Remind them of the key features of an opinion essay.

Think Aloud The best way to persuade readers to agree with your opinion is to support it with enough strong text evidence. Gather details and examples from *Fly, Eagle, Fly!* and "Purple Coyote." You may also use details and examples from your own and others' experiences.

Getting Started Tell students to begin writing their opinion essay using their charts to help them. Give them suggestions about organizing their reasons, facts, and details in logical ways. Brainstorm linking words and phrases, such as *because* and *in addition,* and persuasive words, such as *help* and *important,* that they can use in their writing. Emphasize the importance of using correct grammar and complete sentences. Remind students to end their opinion essay with a concluding statement or section that restates their opinion and reasons for readers to remember.

STEP 4 Evaluate Your Writing

Display the checklist below and have students use it to evaluate their opinion essays. Circulate around the room and confer with individual students.

- ✓ Did I introduce my topic at the beginning?
- ✓ Did I state my opinion clearly?
- ✓ Do my reasons support my opinion?
- ✓ Did I list my reasons using a structure that makes sense?
- ✓ Did I use linking words to connect my opinion and reasons and persuasive words to make my writing more convincing?
- ✓ Does my concluding statement or section sum up my opinion and reasons?

Help students set goals and make a plan for improving in areas where their writing needs help.

STEP 5 Revise and Publish

Help students follow through with their plans for revision. If time permits, have students trade opinion essays and offer one another suggestions for how to improve the writing.

Publishing Students can publish their opinion essays by printing them and presenting them as speeches to the class.

Letter to the Editor

Objectives

- Identify the characteristics of a letter to the editor.
- Write a letter to the editor, using facts and supporting details.
- Evaluate your writing.
- Revise and publish your writing.

 Common Core State Standards

Writing 1. Write opinion pieces on topics or texts, supporting a point of view with reasons. **Writing 1.a.** Introduce the topic or text they are writing about, state an opinion, and create an organizational structure that lists reasons. **Writing 1.b.** Provide reasons that support the opinion. **Writing 1.c.** Use linking words and phrases (e.g., *because, therefore, since, for example*) to connect opinion and reasons. **Writing 1.d.** Provide a concluding statement or section.

STEP 1 Read Like a Writer

Review the key features of a letter to the editor listed below. Respond to any questions students might have.

Key Features of a Letter to the Editor

- States the issue and the writer's point of view about the issue
- Supports the point of view with reasons, facts, and examples
- Organizes reasons using a structure such as order of importance
- Uses persuasive words to appeal to readers' beliefs and emotions
- Provides a concluding statement or section
- Uses the correct format for a letter

Choose a letter to the editor that students have already read to model key features. Display the model for students to see and point out each of the key features.

STEP 2 Organize Your Ideas

Writing Prompt Look back at "Clothes: Bringing Cultures Together" and "Communities Celebrate Cultures." Write a letter to the editor on this issue: "The contributions of many other cultures have made American culture more interesting." Do you agree or disagree? State your point of view and then support it with evidence from both texts.

Think Aloud Your letter to the editor will better persuade readers if your ideas are well organized and clearly presented. First decide which point of view you choose. Then look for reasons, facts, and examples in the texts that you can use to support your point of view. You may wish to make an outline before you begin writing.

Guided Writing Show students how to fill in an outline with their ideas. Explain that when they write their letters to the editor, they will first state their point of view on the issue, present their reasons in a logical order, and end with a statement that restates their point of view and reasons.

STEP 3 Draft Your Writing

Have students use their outlines to write a letter to the editor. Remind them of the key features of a letter to the editor.

Think Aloud The best way to persuade readers to agree with your point of view on an issue is to offer strong reasons and support them with valid facts and details. Gather information from the texts "Clothes: Bringing Cultures Together" and "Communities Celebrate Cultures." You can also look through books, articles, and Web sites to find additional supporting information.

Getting Started Tell students to begin writing their letters to the editor using their outlines. Brainstorm persuasive words, such as *best, worst, always, never, fair, unfair, need, should,* and *important,* that they can use in their writing. Tell students to end their letters to the editor with a concluding statement or section that restates their point of view and reasons so that readers will remember them. Remind students that they should use the correct format for a letter, which includes the date, a greeting, a closing, and a signature.

STEP 4 Evaluate Your Writing

Display the checklist below and have students use it to evaluate their letters to the editor. Circulate around the room and confer with individual students.

- ✓ Did I introduce the issue at the beginning?
- ✓ Did I state my point of view on the issue clearly?
- ✓ Do my reasons, facts, and examples support my point of view?
- ✓ Did I organize my ideas using a structure that makes sense?
- ✓ Did I use persuasive words to appeal to readers?
- ✓ Did I use the correct format for a letter?

Help students set goals and make a plan for improving their writing.

STEP 5 Revise and Publish

Help students follow through with their plans for revision. If time permits, have students trade letters to the editor and offer one another suggestions for how to improve the writing.

Publishing Students can publish their letters to the editor by submitting them to the school newspaper or to a community publication.

Advertisement

Objectives

- Identify the characteristics of an advertisement.
- Write an advertisement, using facts and supporting details.
- Evaluate your writing.
- Revise and publish your writing.

 Common Core State Standards

Writing 1. Write opinion pieces on topics or texts, supporting a point of view with reasons. **Writing 1.a.** Introduce the topic or text they are writing about, state an opinion, and create an organizational structure that lists reasons. **Writing 1.b.** Provide reasons that support the opinion. **Writing 1.c.** Use linking words and phrases (e.g., *because, therefore, since, for example*) to connect opinion and reasons. **Writing 1.d.** Provide a concluding statement or section.

STEP 1 Read Like a Writer

Review the key features of an advertisement listed below. Respond to any questions students might have.

Key Features of an Advertisement
- States the writer's opinion, or claim
- Supports the claim with facts, details, and examples
- Organizes the information in an easy-to-read format
- Uses persuasive words to make the claim more convincing
- Includes graphics such as photographs or illustrations
- Provides a concluding statement or section

Bring in an advertisement to model key features. Display the model for students to see and point out each of the key features you have discussed.

STEP 2 Organize Your Ideas

Writing Prompt Look back at *Jalapeño Bagels* and "Foods of Mexico: A Delicious Blend." Both selections describe baked goods such as challah, bagels, and *bolillos.* Write an advertisement for a bakery. Persuade people that they should come to the bakery to buy the breads, rolls, and other baked goods. Use evidence from both texts to support your opinion, or claim.

Think Aloud Your advertisement will be more persuasive if you organize and present your ideas clearly. First decide how you will state your claim in a way that draws readers in. Then choose the facts, details, and examples from the selections that you will use to support your claim. Review each selection and make a list before you begin writing.

Guided Writing Show students how to make lists of relevant information. Write the title of each selection and details about baked goods from its text and illustrations. Explain to students that when they write their advertisement, they will first state their claim about the bakery; then present their supporting facts, details, and examples in a way that will appeal to readers; and finally close with a statement that sums up why people should come to the bakery.

STEP 3 Draft Your Writing

Have students use their lists to write an advertisement. Remind them of the key features of an advertisement.

Think Aloud How can you persuade readers to come to the bakery? Give them facts, details, and examples that will make them want to buy their baked goods there. Make lists of details about the baked goods in *Jalapeño Bagels* and "Foods of Mexico: A Delicious Blend." You can also list details and ideas from your own experiences and from your imagination.

Getting Started Tell students to begin writing their advertisements using their lists to help them. Discuss how they can organize their facts and details in a way that is easy to read and understand. Brainstorm persuasive words, such as *tasty, fresh, homemade, free,* and *healthy,* that they can use to make their writing more convincing. Emphasize the importance of using correct grammar and complete sentences. Remind students to end their advertisements with a concluding statement or section that sums up what they want readers to do and why. Suggest that they include graphics, such as illustrations, and design elements, such as different font sizes, to help make their advertisements eye-catching.

STEP 4 Evaluate Your Writing

Display the checklist below and have students use it to evaluate their advertisements. Circulate around the room and confer with individual students.

- ✓ Did I state my opinion, or claim, clearly?
- ✓ Do the facts, details, and examples support my claim?
- ✓ Is the information organized in an easy-to-read format?
- ✓ Did I use persuasive words to make my claim more convincing?
- ✓ Did I use graphics that help support the text?
- ✓ Does my concluding statement or section sum up my claim and evidence?

Help students set goals and make a plan for improving in areas where their writing needs help.

STEP 5 Revise and Publish

Help students follow through with their plans for revision. If time permits, have students trade advertisements and offer suggestions for how to improve the writing and layout.

Publishing Students can publish their advertisements by posting them on a bulletin board for classmates and others to see.

More Connect the Texts
Text Review

Objectives

- Identify the characteristics of a text review.
- Write a text review, using facts and supporting details.
- Evaluate your writing.
- Revise and publish your writing.

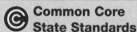

Common Core State Standards

Writing 1. Write opinion pieces on topics or texts, supporting a point of view with reasons. **Writing 1.a.** Introduce the topic or text they are writing about, state an opinion, and create an organizational structure that lists reasons. **Writing 1.b.** Provide reasons that support the opinion. **Writing 1.c.** Use linking words and phrases (e.g., *because, therefore, since, for example*) to connect opinion and reasons. **Writing 1.d.** Provide a concluding statement or section.

STEP 1 Read Like a Writer

Review the key features of a text review listed below. Respond to any questions students might have.

Key Features of a Text Review

- Introduces the topic and states the writer's opinion about the topic
- Supports the opinion with reasons
- Supports the reasons with facts and details from the texts
- Organizes reasons using a structure such as similarities and differences
- Uses linking words and phrases to connect the opinion and reasons
- Provides a concluding statement or section

Choose a review that students have already read to model key features. Display the model for students to see and point out each of the key features you have discussed.

STEP 2 Organize Your Ideas

Writing Prompt Look back at "A Nation of Immigrants" and "Once Upon a Constitution." Both selections are expository texts. Write a review that tells which selection you like better and why. State your opinion and then support it with evidence from both texts.

Think Aloud Your writing will be more persuasive if you organize and present your ideas clearly. Decide what opinion you will state in your review and your reasons for it. Then choose facts, details, and examples from the texts that you will use to support your reasons. Review each text and make a concept web before you begin writing.

Guided Writing Show students how to make a concept web. Write the title of each selection in the center circle and details from the selections in the outer circles. Explain to students that when they write their review, they can use this information to briefly summarize the two selections. Then they will state their opinion, present their reasons in a logical order, and end with a statement that sums up their opinion and reasons.

STEP 3 Draft Your Writing

Have students use their concept webs to write a text review. Remind them of the key features of a text review.

Think Aloud How can you persuade readers to agree with your opinion? Give them reasons, facts, and details that clearly support your point of view. Use the ideas from your concept webs to remind you about details in the selections "A Nation of Immigrants" and "Once Upon a Constitution."

Getting Started Tell students to begin writing their text review using their concept webs to help them stay on topic. Offer suggestions about organizing their reasons, facts, and details in logical ways. Brainstorm linking words and phrases, such as *therefore* and *as a result,* that they can use to connect their opinion and reasons. Emphasize the importance of using correct grammar and complete sentences. Remind students to end their text reviews with a concluding statement or section that restates their opinion and reasons.

STEP 4 Evaluate Your Writing

Display the checklist below and have students use it to evaluate their text reviews. Circulate around the room and confer with individual students.

✓ Did I introduce my topic at the beginning?

✓ Did I state my opinion clearly?

✓ Do my reasons support my opinion?

✓ Did I use text evidence to support my reasons?

✓ Did I use linking words and phrases to connect my opinion and reasons?

✓ Does my concluding statement sum up my opinion and reasons?

Help students set goals and make a plan for improving in areas where their writing needs help.

STEP 5 Revise and Publish

Help students follow through with their plans for revision. If time permits, have students trade text reviews and offer suggestions for how to improve the writing.

Publishing Students can publish their text reviews by compiling them to make a print or online review magazine.

More Connect the Texts
Opinion Essay

Objectives

- Identify the characteristics of an opinion essay.
- Write an opinion essay, using facts and supporting details.
- Evaluate your writing.
- Revise and publish your writing.

 Common Core State Standards

Writing 1. Write opinion pieces on topics or texts, supporting a point of view with reasons. **Writing 1.a.** Introduce the topic or text they are writing about, state an opinion, and create an organizational structure that lists reasons. **Writing 1.b.** Provide reasons that support the opinion. **Writing 1.c.** Use linking words and phrases (e.g., *because, therefore, since, for example*) to connect opinion and reasons. **Writing 1.d.** Provide a concluding statement or section.

STEP 1 Read Like a Writer

Review the key features of an opinion essay listed below. Respond to any questions students might have.

Key Features of an Opinion Essay

- Introduces the topic and states the writer's opinion about the topic
- Supports the opinion with reasons
- Organizes reasons using a structure such as order of importance
- Uses linking words and phrases to connect the opinion and reasons
- Uses persuasive words to make writing more convincing
- Provides a concluding statement or section

Choose an opinion essay that students have already read to model key features. Display the model for students to see and point out each of the key features you have discussed.

STEP 2 Organize Your Ideas

Writing Prompt Look back at *Happy Birthday Mr. Kang* and *Talking Walls: Art for the People.* Both texts describe people who create literature and art. Write an opinion essay on this topic: "People need literature and art in their lives." Do you agree or disagree? State your opinion and then support it with evidence from both texts.

Think Aloud Your ideas will be more persuasive if they are well organized and clearly presented. First decide what opinion you will state in your essay. Then choose the reasons, facts, details, and examples from the texts that you will use to support your opinion. You may wish to make an outline before you begin writing.

Guided Writing Display a simple outline. Show students how to write their opinion on the title line; their reasons on the I, II, and III lines; and the facts and details that support each reason on the A, B, and C lines below each Roman numeral. Explain to students that when they write their essays, they will first state their opinion, present their reasons in a logical order, and then end with a statement that sums up their opinion and reasons.

STEP 3 Draft Your Writing

Have students use their outlines to write an opinion essay. Remind them of the key features of an opinion essay.

Think Aloud The best way to persuade readers to agree with your opinion is to support it with strong evidence. Gather details and examples from *Happy Birthday Mr. Kang* and *Talking Walls: Art for the People.* You may also use details and examples from other articles you have read.

Getting Started Tell students to begin writing their opinion essays using their outlines to help them. Give them suggestions about organizing their reasons, facts, and details in logical ways. Brainstorm linking words and phrases, such as *because* and *in addition,* and persuasive words, such as *necessary* and *important,* that they can use in their writing. Emphasize the importance of using correct grammar and complete sentences. Remind students to end their opinion essays with a concluding statement or section that restates their opinion and reasons for readers to remember.

STEP 4 Evaluate Your Writing

Display the checklist below and have students use it to evaluate their opinion essays. Circulate around the room and confer with individual students.

✓ Did I introduce my topic at the beginning?

✓ Did I state my opinion clearly?

✓ Do my reasons support my opinion?

✓ Did I list my reasons using a structure that makes sense?

✓ Did I use linking words to connect my opinion and reasons and persuasive words to make my writing more convincing?

✓ Does my concluding statement or section sum up my opinion and reasons?

Help students set goals and make a plan for improving in areas where their writing needs help.

STEP 5 Revise and Publish

Help students follow through with their plans for revision. If time permits, have students trade opinion essays and offer one another suggestions for how to improve the writing.

Publishing Students can publish their opinion essays by taking turns presenting them orally to their classmates.

Persuasive Speech

Objectives

- Identify the characteristics of a persuasive speech.
- Write a persuasive speech, using facts and supporting details.
- Evaluate your writing.
- Revise and publish your writing.

Ⓒ Common Core State Standards

Writing 1. Write opinion pieces on topics or texts, supporting a point of view with reasons. **Writing 1.a.** Introduce the topic or text they are writing about, state an opinion, and create an organizational structure that lists reasons. **Writing 1.b.** Provide reasons that support the opinion. **Writing 1.c.** Use linking words and phrases (e.g., *because, therefore, since, for example*) to connect opinion and reasons. **Writing 1.d.** Provide a concluding statement or section.

STEP 1 Read Like a Writer

Review the key features of a persuasive speech listed below. Respond to any questions students might have.

Key Features of a Persuasive Speech

- Introduces the issue and states the writer's point of view about the issue
- Supports the point of view with reasons, facts, and examples
- Organizes reasons using a structure such as order of importance
- Uses persuasive words to make ideas more convincing to listeners
- Provides a concluding statement or section

Choose a persuasive speech or another opinion piece that students have already read to model key features. Display the model for students to see and point out each of the key features you have discussed.

STEP 2 Organize Your Ideas

Writing Prompt Look back at *Happy Birthday Mr. Kang* and "The Monster in the Maze." Both texts have something to say about living things and freedom. Write a persuasive speech on this issue: "All living things should be free." Do you agree or disagree? State your point of view and then support it with evidence from both texts.

Think Aloud Your speech will be more persuasive if your ideas are well organized and clearly presented. First decide what your point of view on the issue is. Then look for reasons, facts, details, and examples in the texts that you can use to support your point of view. You may wish to make an outline before you begin writing.

Guided Writing Display an outline. Remind students how to write the issue and their point of view about the issue on the title line; their reasons on the I, II, and III lines; and the text evidence that supports each reason on the A, B, and C lines below each Roman numeral. Explain to students that when they write their persuasive speech, they will first state their point of view on the issue, then present their reasons in a logical order, and end with a statement that restates their point of view and reasons.

STEP 3 Draft Your Writing

Have students use their outlines to write a persuasive speech. Remind them of the key features of a persuasive speech.

Think Aloud The best way to persuade listeners to agree with a point of view on an issue is to offer strong reasons and support them with valid reasons, facts, and details. You can gather information from the texts *Happy Birthday Mr. Kang* and "The Monster in the Maze" to support your point of view.

Getting Started Tell students to begin writing their persuasive speech using their outlines to help them. Give them suggestions about organizing their reasons, facts, and details in logical ways. Brainstorm persuasive words, such as *best, always, never, fair, terrible, right,* and *wrong,* that they can use in their speech. Emphasize the importance of using correct grammar and complete sentences. Remind students to end their persuasive speech with a concluding statement or section that restates their point of view.

STEP 4 Evaluate Your Writing

Display the checklist below and have students use it to evaluate their persuasive speeches. Circulate around the room and confer with individual students.

✓ Did I introduce the issue at the beginning?

✓ Did I state my point of view on the issue clearly?

✓ Do my reasons, facts, and examples support my point of view?

✓ Did I organize my ideas using a structure that makes sense?

✓ Did I use persuasive words to appeal to listeners?

✓ Does my concluding statement restate my point of view and reasons?

Help students set goals and make a plan for improving in areas where their writing needs help.

STEP 5 Revise and Publish

Help students follow through with their plans for revision. If time permits, have students trade persuasive speeches and offer suggestions for how to improve the writing.

Publishing Students can publish their persuasive speeches by presenting them in front of the class or a small group.

More Connect the Texts
Report

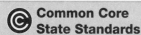
STEP 1 Read Like a Writer

Review the key features of a report listed below. Respond to any questions students might have.

Key Features of a Report
- Introduces the topic at the beginning
- Develops the topic with facts, definitions, and details
- Groups related facts, definitions, and details together
- Uses linking words and phrases to connect ideas
- Provides a concluding statement or section

Choose an informative/explanatory text that students have already read to model key features. Display the model for students to see and point out each of the key features you have discussed.

STEP 2 Organize Your Ideas

Writing Prompt Look back at *When Charlie McButton Lost Power* and "How a Kite Changed the World." The first text describes the many ways Charlie McButton uses electricity in his daily life. The second text discusses how Benjamin Franklin used electricity in his time. Write a report that tells about the different ways people use electricity. Provide evidence from both texts to develop your topic.

Think Aloud Readers will understand your ideas better if they are well organized. Decide on the main idea of your report. Then choose facts, definitions, and details from the texts to support your main idea. You can use a main idea and details chart to organize your ideas before you begin writing.

Guided Writing Display a chart with a big box at the top and several smaller boxes below it. Show students how to write their main idea in the top box and the facts and details that support their main idea in the other boxes. Explain to students that when they write their report, they will first state their main idea, then arrange their supporting details in a logical order, and finally end with a statement or section that sums up the ideas they presented.

STEP 3 Draft Your Writing

Have students use their charts to write a report. Remind them of the key features of a report.

Think Aloud The main purpose of a report is to present facts and details about a topic. You can find facts and details to use in your report by rereading *When Charlie McButton Lost Power* and "How a Kite Changed the World." You can also do research using books, articles, and Web sites to find additional facts about your topic.

Getting Started Tell students to begin writing their report using their charts to keep them focused on their topic. Give them suggestions on how to group related information and how to arrange the information in a logical order. Brainstorm words and phrases that students can use to link their ideas, for example, *also, and, but,* and *or.* Emphasize the importance of using correct grammar and complete sentences. Remind students to end their report with a concluding statement or section that sums up their ideas but does not introduce any new ideas.

STEP 4 Evaluate Your Writing

Display the checklist below and have students use it to evaluate their reports. Circulate around the room and confer with individual students.

- ✓ Did I introduce my topic at the beginning?
- ✓ Did I state my topic clearly?
- ✓ Do my facts and details support my main idea?
- ✓ Did I organize my information in a logical way?
- ✓ Did I use linking words and phrases to make connections between my ideas?
- ✓ Does my concluding statement or section sum up my ideas without introducing new ideas?

Help students set goals and make a plan for improving in areas where their writing needs help.

STEP 5 Revise and Publish

Help students follow through with their plans for revision. If time permits, have students trade reports and offer suggestions for how to improve the writing.

Publishing Students can publish their reports by taking turns presenting them orally to the class.

More Connect the Texts
Interview

© Common Core State Standards

Writing 2. Write informative/ explanatory texts to examine a topic and convey ideas and information clearly. **Writing 2.a.** Introduce a topic and group related information together; include illustrations when useful to aiding comprehension. **Writing 2.b.** Develop the topic with facts, definitions, and details. **Writing 2.c.** Use linking words and phrases (e.g., *also, another, and, more, but*) to connect ideas within categories of information. **Writing 2.d.** Provide a concluding statement or section.

STEP 1 Read Like a Writer

Review the key features of an interview listed below. Respond to any questions students might have.

Key Features of an Interview

- Introduces the interviewer, topic, and people being interviewed
- Develops the topic through interviewer's questions and people's answers
- Uses facts, definitions, and details in answers to questions
- Presents questions and answers in a logical order
- Provides a concluding section

Choose an informative/explanatory text that students have already read to model key features. Display the model for students to see and point out each of the key features you have discussed.

STEP 2 Organize Your Ideas

Writing Prompt Look back at *Kumak's Fish* and "How to Catch a Fish." Both texts tell about people fishing. Write an interview with Kumak and Vicki Edwards. Ask them questions about fishing and then answer the questions for them. Use facts and details from both texts to develop your questions and answers.

Think Aloud Like all forms of expository writing, an interview has a main idea. Decide what the main idea of your interview is. Then reread the two texts looking for facts, definitions, and details that are related to that main idea. Think of interview questions you can answer using the information you find. You can use index cards to organize your ideas before you begin writing.

Guided Writing Display several index cards. Show students how to write each question and answer on a card. Explain to students that they should first read through the cards and choose the best questions and answers to use in their interview. Then they can arrange those cards in the order they think is best. Point out that they need to include an introduction that identifies the interviewer, the topic, and the people being interviewed and a conclusion that sums up what was said and ends the interview.

STEP 3 Draft Your Writing

Have students use their index cards to write an interview. Remind them of the key features of an interview.

Think Aloud The main purpose of an interview is to present facts and details about a topic. You can find facts and details to use in your interview by rereading *Kumak's Fish* and "How to Catch a Fish." You can also look at books, articles, and Web sites to find additional information about your topic.

Getting Started Tell students to begin their interview by writing an opening in which they introduce themselves as the interviewer, tell the topic of the interview, and introduce the people being interviewed. Remind students to use their index cards to write the questions and answers as the body of their interview. Emphasize the importance of using correct grammar and complete sentences. Remind students to end with a concluding section that sums up what the people said and lets readers know that the interview is over.

STEP 4 Evaluate Your Writing

Display the checklist below and have students use it to evaluate their interviews. Circulate around the room and confer with individual students.

- ✓ Did I include an introduction in the interview?
- ✓ Does the introduction identify my role, the topic, and the people being interviewed?
- ✓ Did I organize the questions and answers in a logical way?
- ✓ Do the questions address the topic and the main idea?
- ✓ Did I use facts, definitions, and details in the answers?
- ✓ Does the concluding section sum up what was said in the interview?

Help students set goals and make a plan for improving in areas where their writing needs help.

STEP 5 Revise and Publish

Help students follow through with their plans for revision. If time permits, have students trade interviews and offer suggestions for how to improve the writing.

Publishing Students can publish their interviews by enlisting the help of two classmates and presenting the interview as a skit in front of the class.

Compare-and-Contrast Essay

STEP 1   Read Like a Writer

Review the key features of a compare-and-contrast essay listed below. Respond to any questions students might have.

Key Features of a Compare-and-Contrast Essay

- Introduces the topic at the beginning
- Develops the topic with facts and details drawn from the texts
- Organizes information using a structure such as similarities first, then differences
- Uses linking words and phrases to signal similarities and differences
- Provides a concluding statement or section

Choose a compare-and-contrast essay or another informative/ explanatory text that students have already read to model key features. Display the model for students to see and point out each of the key features you have discussed.

STEP 2   Organize Your Ideas

Writing Prompt Look back at *Tops & Bottoms* and "The Hare and the Tortoise." Both stories feature hares as main characters. Write an essay in which you compare and contrast these two characters. Tell how they are alike and how they are different. Provide evidence from both texts to develop your topic.

Think Aloud Readers will understand your ideas better if they are well organized. First decide how you will state the topic of your compare-and-contrast essay. Then look for facts and details from the texts to support the topic. You can use a Venn diagram to help you organize your ideas before you begin writing.

Guided Writing Display a Venn diagram. Show students how to label each circle with a character's name and then write details about the characters in the circles. Similarities are written in the center section; differences are written in the outer parts of the circles. Explain to students that when they write their compare-and-contrast essay, they will first state their topic, then arrange their facts and details in a logical order, and finally end with a statement that sums up the ideas they presented.

STEP 3 Draft Your Writing

Have students use their Venn diagrams to write a compare-and-contrast essay. Remind them of the key features of a compare-and-contrast essay.

Think Aloud The main purpose of a compare-and-contrast essay is to tell how two things are alike and different. To find similarities and differences to use in your essay, reread *Tops & Bottoms* and "The Hare and the Tortoise." Make a list of facts and details about each hare using the text and illustrations in the stories. Then compare your two lists.

Getting Started Tell students to begin writing their compare-and-contrast essay using their Venn diagrams to stay focused on their topic. Give them suggestions about how to group related information, for example, putting similarities in one paragraph and differences in another paragraph. Brainstorm linking words, such as *and, also, both, but,* and *however,* that students can use to indicate comparisons and contrasts. Emphasize the importance of using correct grammar and complete sentences. Remind students to end their compare-and-contrast essay with a concluding statement or section that sums up their ideas.

STEP 4 Evaluate Your Writing

Display the checklist below and have students use it to evaluate their compare-and-contrast essays. Circulate around the room and confer with individual students.

- ✓ Did I state my topic clearly at the beginning?
- ✓ Do my facts and details support my topic?
- ✓ Did I organize my information in a logical way?
- ✓ Did I use linking words and phrases to show comparisons and contrasts?
- ✓ Does my concluding statement or section sum up my ideas?

Help students set goals and make a plan for improving in areas where their writing needs help.

STEP 5 Revise and Publish

Help students follow through with their plans for revision. If time permits, have students trade compare-and-contrast essays and offer suggestions for how to improve the writing.

Publishing Students can publish their compare-and-contrast essays by taking turns presenting them orally to the class.

More Connect the Texts
Explanation

Objectives

- Identify the characteristics of an explanation.
- Write an explanation, using facts and supporting details.
- Evaluate your writing.
- Revise and publish your writing.

 Common Core State Standards

Writing 2. Write informative/ explanatory texts to examine a topic and convey ideas and information clearly. **Writing 2.a.** Introduce a topic and group related information together; include illustrations when useful to aiding comprehension. **Writing 2.b.** Develop the topic with facts, definitions, and details. **Writing 2.c.** Use linking words and phrases (e.g., *also, another, and, more, but*) to connect ideas within categories of information. **Writing 2.d.** Provide a concluding statement or section.

STEP 1 Read Like a Writer

Review the key features of an explanation listed below. Respond to any questions students might have.

Key Features of an Explanation

- Introduces the topic at the beginning
- Develops the topic with facts, definitions, and details
- Groups related facts, definitions, and details together
- Uses linking words and phrases to connect ideas
- Provides a concluding statement or section

Choose an explanation that students have already read to model key features. Display the model for students to see and point out each of the key features you have discussed.

STEP 2 Organize Your Ideas

Writing Prompt Look back at "Worms at Work" and "The Water Cycle." Why are the graphics and organization particularly important to these selections? Write an explanation that answers this question. Provide evidence from both texts to develop your topic.

Think Aloud Readers will understand your ideas better if they are well organized. Decide how you will state the topic of your explanation. Then choose facts, definitions, details, and examples from the texts to support the topic. You can use a chart to organize your ideas before you begin writing.

Guided Writing Display a two-column chart. Show students how to write their topic above the chart and the selection titles as column headings. In each column, write several facts and details about the selection's graphics and organization that support their topic. Explain to students that when they write their explanations, they will first state their topic, arrange their supporting evidence in a logical order, and finally end with a statement or section that sums up the ideas they presented.

STEP 3 Draft Your Writing

Have students use their charts to write an explanation. Remind them of the key features of an explanation.

Think Aloud The main purpose of an explanation is to give reasons for something or to make something clear by presenting facts and details. Reread "Worms at Work" and "The Water Cycle," looking for facts and details to use in your explanation. You can also look for additional ideas in books and articles and on Web sites.

Getting Started Tell students to begin writing their explanations using their charts to keep them focused on their topic. Give them suggestions on how to group related information and how to arrange the information in a logical order. Brainstorm words and phrases that students can use to link their ideas, for example, *also, and, but,* and *or.* Emphasize the importance of using correct grammar and complete sentences. Remind students to end their explanation with a concluding statement or section that sums up their ideas.

STEP 4 Evaluate Your Writing

Display the checklist below and have students use it to evaluate their explanations. Circulate around the room and confer with individual students.

- ✓ Did I introduce my topic at the beginning?
- ✓ Did I state my topic clearly?
- ✓ Do my facts and details support my main idea?
- ✓ Did I organize my information in a logical way?
- ✓ Did I use linking words and phrases to make connections between my ideas?
- ✓ Does my concluding statement or section sum up my ideas?

Help students set goals and make a plan for improving in areas where their writing needs help.

STEP 5 Revise and Publish

Help students follow through with their plans for revision. If time permits, have students trade explanations and offer suggestions for how to improve the writing.

Publishing Students can print their explanations and take turns presenting them orally to the class.

More Connect the Texts
How-to Report

STEP 1 Read Like a Writer

Review the key features of a how-to report listed below. Respond to any questions students might have.

Key Features of a How-to Report

- Introduces an activity at the beginning
- Explains the activity as a step-by-step process
- Use facts, definitions, and details to fully describe the steps
- Uses time-order words and phrases to indicate the sequence of the steps
- Provides a concluding statement or section

Choose a how-to report or other procedural text that students have already read to model key features. Display the model for students to see and point out each of the key features you have discussed.

STEP 2 Organize Your Ideas

Writing Prompt Look back at *Rocks in His Head* and "Marvelous Marble Mania." Both selections tell about people gathering collections of favorite objects. Write a how-to report that explains how a person could start a collection. Provide evidence from both texts to develop your topic.

Think Aloud Readers will understand your ideas better if they are well organized. Decide how you will state the topic of your how-to report. Then choose facts, definitions, and details from the texts that will help you tell the steps in the activity. You can use a sequence chart to organize your ideas before you begin writing.

Guided Writing Display a chart with six or more boxes in a vertical column. Show students how to write their topic in the top box and the facts and details for the steps in the other boxes. Explain to students that when they write their how-to report, they will first state their topic, or the activity they are explaining. Then they will write the steps in the order they should be done, making sure to include all necessary details and information. Finally, they will end with a statement or section that wraps up the activity they are explaining.

STEP 3 Draft Your Writing

Have students use their sequence charts to write a how-to report. Remind them of the key features of a how-to report.

Think Aloud The main purpose of a how-to report is to explain how to do the steps in a process. You can find facts and details to use in your how-to report by rereading *Rocks in His Head* and "Marvelous Marble Mania." You can also use facts and details from your own or others' collecting experiences or from research using books, articles, and Web sites.

Getting Started Tell students to begin writing their how-to report using their charts to help them focus on their topic. Give them suggestions on how to group related information into steps and how to arrange the steps in a logical order. Brainstorm words and phrases, such as *first, next, last, after, before,* and *finally,* that students can use to clearly show the sequence of the steps. Emphasize the importance of using correct grammar and complete sentences. Remind students to end their how-to report with a concluding statement or section that wraps up the activity.

STEP 4 Evaluate Your Writing

Display the checklist below and have students use it to evaluate their how-to reports. Circulate around the room and confer with individual students.

✓ Did I introduce my activity at the beginning?

✓ Did I explain the activity in a series of steps?

✓ Did I give enough information to make each step clear?

✓ Did I use time-order words and phrases to clarify the sequence of the steps?

✓ Does my concluding statement or section sum up the activity?

Help students set goals and make a plan for improving in areas where their writing needs help.

STEP 5 Revise and Publish

Help students follow through with their plans for revision. If time permits, have students trade how-to reports and offer suggestions for how to improve the writing.

Publishing Students can publish their how-to reports by sharing them with classmates, friends, and family members.

Compare-and-Contrast Essay

Objectives

- Identify the characteristics of a compare-and-contrast essay.
- Write a compare-and-contrast essay, using facts and details.
- Evaluate your writing.
- Revise and publish your writing.

Common Core State Standards

Writing 2. Write informative/explanatory texts to examine a topic and convey ideas and information clearly. **Writing 2.a.** Introduce a topic and group related information together; include illustrations when useful to aiding comprehension. **Writing 2.b.** Develop the topic with facts, definitions, and details. **Writing 2.c.** Use linking words and phrases (e.g., *also, another, and, more, but*) to connect ideas within categories of information. **Writing 2.d.** Provide a concluding statement or section.

STEP 1 Read Like a Writer

Review the key features of a compare-and-contrast essay listed below. Respond to any questions students might have.

Key Features of a Compare-and-Contrast Essay

- Introduces the topic at the beginning
- Develops the topic with facts and details drawn from the texts
- Organizes information using a structure such as similarities first, then differences
- Uses linking words and phrases to signal similarities and differences
- Provides a concluding statement or section

Choose a compare-and-contrast essay or another informative/explanatory text that students have already read to model key features. Display the model for students to see and point out each of the key features you have discussed.

STEP 2 Organize Your Ideas

Writing Prompt Look back at *Suki's Kimono* and *Jalapeño Bagels.* The main characters are children who show how they feel about their families' cultures. Write an essay in which you compare and contrast these two characters. Tell how they are alike and how they are different. Provide evidence from both texts to develop your topic.

Think Aloud Readers will understand your ideas better if they are well organized. First decide how you will state the topic of your compare-and-contrast essay. Then look for facts and details from the texts to support the topic. You can use a Venn diagram to help you organize your ideas before you begin writing.

Guided Writing Display a Venn diagram. Show students how to label each circle with a character's name and then write details about the characters in the circles. Similarities are written in the center section; differences are written in the outer parts of the circles. Explain to students that when they write their compare-and-contrast essays, they will first state their topic, arrange their facts and details in a logical order, and finally end with a statement that sums up the ideas they presented.

STEP 3 Draft Your Writing

Have students use their Venn diagrams to write a compare-and-contrast essay. Remind them of the key features of a compare-and-contrast essay.

Think Aloud The main purpose of a compare-and-contrast essay is to tell how two people or things are alike and different. To find similarities and differences to use in your essay, reread *Suki's Kimono* and *Jalapeño Bagels*. Using the text and illustrations in the story, make a list of facts and details about each main character. Then compare your two lists.

Getting Started Tell students to begin writing their compare-and-contrast essay using their Venn diagrams to stay focused on their topic. Give them suggestions about how to group related information, for example, putting similarities in one paragraph and differences in another paragraph. Brainstorm linking words, such as *and, also, both, but,* and *however,* that students can use to indicate comparisons and contrasts. Emphasize the importance of using correct grammar and complete sentences. Remind students to end their compare-and-contrast essay with a concluding statement or section that sums up their ideas.

STEP 4 Evaluate Your Writing

Display the checklist below and have students use it to evaluate their compare-and-contrast essays. Circulate around the room and confer with individual students.

- ✓ Did I state my topic clearly at the beginning?
- ✓ Do my facts and details support my topic?
- ✓ Did I organize my information in a logical way?
- ✓ Did I use linking words and phrases to show comparisons and contrasts?
- ✓ Does my concluding statement or section sum up my ideas?

Help students set goals and make a plan for improving in areas where their writing needs help.

STEP 5 Revise and Publish

Help students follow through with their plans for revision. If time permits, have students trade compare-and-contrast essays and offer suggestions for how to improve the writing.

Publishing Students can publish their compare-and-contrast essays by printing them and taking turns presenting them orally to the class.

More Connect the Texts
Research Report

Objectives

- Identify the characteristics of a research report.
- Write a research report, using facts and supporting details.
- Evaluate your writing.
- Revise and publish your writing.

Common Core State Standards

Writing 2. Write informative/explanatory texts to examine a topic and convey ideas and information clearly. **Writing 2.a.** Introduce a topic and group related information together; include illustrations when useful to aiding comprehension. **Writing 2.b.** Develop the topic with facts, definitions, and details. **Writing 2.c.** Use linking words and phrases (e.g., *also, another, and, more, but*) to connect ideas within categories of information. **Writing 2.d.** Provide a concluding statement or section.

STEP 1 Read Like a Writer

Review the key features of a research report listed below. Respond to any questions students might have.

Key Features of a Research Report
- Introduces the topic at the beginning
- Develops the topic with facts, definitions, and details
- Includes information from several sources
- Groups information together in paragraphs
- Uses linking words and phrases to connect ideas
- Provides a concluding statement or section

Choose a research or another kind of informative/explanatory report that students have already read to model key features. Display the model for students to see and point out each of the key features you have discussed.

STEP 2 Organize Your Ideas

Writing Prompt Look back at *Atlantis: The Legend of a Lost City* and "The Monster in the Maze." Both texts are stories that provide information about Crete. Write a research report that tells about Crete. Provide evidence from both texts and from other research to develop your topic.

Think Aloud Readers will understand your ideas better if they are well organized. Decide on the main idea of your research report. Then choose facts, definitions, and details from the texts to support your main idea. You can use a main idea and details chart to organize your ideas before you begin writing.

Guided Writing Display a chart with a large box at the top and several smaller boxes below it. Remind students how to write their main idea in the top box and the facts and details that support their main idea in the other boxes. Explain to students that when they write their research reports, they will first state their main idea, then arrange their supporting details in a logical order, and end with a statement that sums up their ideas.

STEP 3 Draft Your Writing

Have students use their charts to write a research report. Remind them of the key features of a research report.

Think Aloud As with most kinds of reports, the main purpose of a research report is to present facts and details about a topic. First reread *Atlantis: The Legend of a Lost City* and "The Monster in the Maze" to find facts and details about Crete to use in your research report. Then research the topic in books and articles and on Web sites to find more facts and details.

Getting Started Tell students to begin writing their research reports using their charts to help them stay focused on their topic. Give them suggestions on how to group related information into paragraphs and how to arrange the paragraphs in a logical order. Brainstorm words and phrases that students can use to link the ideas in their paragraphs, for example, *also, and, but,* and *or.* Emphasize the importance of using correct grammar and complete sentences. Remind students to end their research reports with a concluding statement or section that sums up their ideas but does not introduce any new ideas.

STEP 4 Evaluate Your Writing

Display the checklist below and have students use it to evaluate their research reports. Circulate around the room and confer with individual students.

✓ Did I state my topic clearly at the beginning?

✓ Do my facts, definitions, and details support my main idea?

✓ Does my information come from several different sources?

✓ Did I use paragraphs to group related information?

✓ Are my paragraphs organized in a logical way?

✓ Did I use linking words and phrases to make connections between ideas?

✓ Does my concluding statement or section sum up my ideas without introducing any new ideas?

Help students set goals and make a plan for improving in areas where their writing needs help.

STEP 5 Revise and Publish

Help students follow through with their plans for revision. If time permits, have students trade research reports and offer suggestions for how to improve the writing.

Publishing Students can publish their research reports by using them as part of a presentation to the class that includes visual and audio aids.